Robert Fergusson
SELECTED POEMS

Robert Ferguson
SELECTED POEMS

Robert Fergusson
SELECTED POEMS

Edited & Introduced by
JAMES ROBERTSON

This edition published in paperback in Great Britain in 2024
by Polygon, an imprint of Birlinn Ltd.

Birlinn Ltd
West Newington House
10 Newington Road
Edinburgh EH9 1QS

www.polygonbooks.co.uk

First published in 2000 with an updated
edition published in 2007. It was reissued in 2017.

Introduction copyright © James Robertson, 2007

All rights reserved.
No part of this publication may be
reproduced, stored, or transmitted in any form, or by
any means, electronic, mechanical or photocopying,
recording or otherwise, without the express
written permission of the publisher.

ISBN 13: 978 1 84697 687 2
eBook ISBN: 978 0 85790 886 5

British Library Cataloguing-in-Publication Data
A catalogue record for this book is available on request
from the British Library.

Typesetting by TexturAL, Dundee
Printed and bound in Great Britain by Ashford Press, Gosport

CONTENTS

Acknowledgements — vii
Introduction — 1
A Note on the Text — 39
Notes on the Illustrations — 43

The Poems (in the order in which they were written)
Elegy, on the Death of Mr David Gregory, Late Professor of Mathematics in the University of St Andrews — 49
The Daft-Days — 52
Elegy, on the Death of Scots Music — 56
The King's Birth-Day in Edinburgh — 59
Caller Oysters — 65

Epistles Between J.S. and Robert Fergusson
  To Mr Robert Fergusson * — 70
  Answer to Mr J.S.'s Epistle — 73
Braid Claith — 77
An Eclogue, to the Memory of Dr William Wilkie, Late Professor of Natural Philosophy in the University of St Andrews — 80
An Eclogue — 84
Hallow-Fair — 89
The Lee-Rigg — 94
To the Tron-Kirk Bell — 95
Caller Water — 98
Auld Reikie — 102
Mutual Complaint of Plainstanes and Causey, in their Mother-tongue — 116

---

* Poems addressed to Fergusson

The Rising of the Session	123
Ode to the Bee	127
The Farmer's Ingle	130
The Ghaists: A Kirk-yard Eclogue	135

Epistles Between Andrew Gray and Robert Fergusson

To R. Fergusson *	141
To Andrew Gray	143
On Seeing a Butterfly in the Street	146
Hame Content: A Satire	149
Leith Races	154
Ode to the Gowdspink	162
To the Principal and Professors of the University of St Andrews, on their Superb Treat to Dr Samuel Johnson	165
The Election	169
Elegy on John Hogg, Late Porter to the University of St Andrews	175
Dumfries	179
The Sitting of the Session	181
A Drink Eclogue: Landlady, Brandy and Whisky	184
To My Auld Breeks	189
Rob. Fergusson's Last Will †	193
Horace, Ode XI. Lib I	196
The Author's Life †	197
On Night †	198
Job, Chapter III, Paraphrased †	199
Glossary	201

* Poems addressed to Fergusson
† Poems in English

Acknowledgements

In preparing this new edition (first published in 2000, revised in 2007) my biggest debt is to the scholars who have worked on Robert Fergusson previously. A brief bibliography of books consulted is given at the end of the Introduction, but my researches have extended far beyond those titles. The two-volume Scottish Text Society edition prepared by Matthew P. McDiarmid in the 1950s remains the most comprehensive and authoritative source of information on both poet and poems. Any modern selection of Fergusson's work must take McDiarmid as its starting-point, and this one is no exception.

As part of the celebrations in 2000 of the 250th anniversary of Fergusson's birth, the St Andrews Scottish Studies Institute at the University of St Andrews organised a series of seminars under the general title 'Heaven-Taught Fergusson'. Useful information and ideas were gained from the talks given by Dr Matthew Simpson on Fergusson and St Andrews student culture, and by Andrew Macintosh on Fergusson and Robert Garioch, and also from discussions with Professor Robert Crawford.

Others to whom I am grateful for help, advice and information include Billy Kay, Annie Matheson, Alan Lawson, Liz Short and Hugh Andrew.

James Robertson
Newtyle, February 2007

Introduction

There is no escaping the tragedy of Robert Fergusson. Scotland has had its share of writers who died far too young: Robert Burns, of course, dead at thirty-seven; Robert Louis Stevenson at forty-four; Lewis Grassic Gibbon at thirty-four; George Douglas Brown, author of *The House with the Green Shutters*, at thirty-three; John MacDougall Hay, who wrote *Gillespie*, at thirty-eight; the novelist Mary Brunton at forty; Fergusson's contemporary the poet Michael Bruce, killed by tuberculosis aged just twenty-one. But the loss of Fergusson at twenty-four seems somehow the most terrible of all. The bleakness of his last months – his descent into mental illness and destitution in the Edinburgh Bedlam – stands in such contrast to the brilliance of the previous two years, when his genius bloomed in a remarkable series of poems, that it almost obscures his achievement.

Certainly it is not difficult to see, in some of Fergusson's lines and phrases, indications of what was to befall him. The riotous humour, the outrageous rhymes and cutting observation of his celebrations of Edinburgh life, are tempered by an awareness of human frailty and transience; "poortith" and sorrow are never far to seek, and behind every joyous drunken scene in inn or oyster-tavern lies a fear of "that dowie dismal house, the grave" ('Ode to the Bee'). Then, too, given the richness of his output in so short a life, it is natural to speculate on what might have been, had he lived only another twelve or fifteen years. Might he have written more for his first love, the theatre? Would he have completed his long work 'Auld Reikie'? At the very least, we may assume he would have met Burns, who would undoubtedly have sought out his "elder brother in the Muse" on arrival in Edinburgh in 1786. What might have resulted from that encounter? In the end, though, we are left with Fergusson's crowning glory, the thirty-odd poems he composed in Scots, and it is for these, above all, that he deserves to be remembered.

Early Life

Robert Fergusson was born in Edinburgh on 5th September 1750 in Cap-and-Feather Close, which ran up to the High Street from the north side, opposite but slightly above Niddry's Wynd (now Niddry Street). The close was demolished in the poet's own lifetime to make way for construction of the North Bridge (1765–72). His parents were both from Aberdeenshire, and had settled in the capital only two years previously. William Fergusson was born in 1713 or 1714, and grew up in the parish of Tarland. In 1740 or 1741 he married Elizabeth Forbes, who was born in 1714. She was the daughter of a gentleman, John Forbes of Templeton, in the parish of Kildrummie. Before moving south, William and Elizabeth had three children, Hary (born 1742), Barbara (born 1744) and John (born 1746, who died in infancy).

Little is known of William Fergusson's family background, which was humble compared with that of Elizabeth Forbes. It appears that he had moved to the city of Aberdeen for work, but some event, perhaps the death of his employer there, induced him to come to Edinburgh, where he worked as a clerk for various businesses. He lacked contacts, and the jobs he found were poorly paid and insecure: it was a struggle to keep his family even in basic necessities, especially after the birth, in 1753, of another daughter, Margaret. Nevertheless, he and his wife were aware of the advantages which education, in the absence of social influence, might give their children: a surviving letter shows that in 1751, when the family's total annual income was less than £20, they managed to put £1 15s towards school fees.[1]

In 1756 William became clerk to Walter Fergusson, Writer to the Signet, a post he held for some six years. William may himself have had some literary talent, as he apparently wrote verses as a young man, but it was Elizabeth who taught young Rob, as he was known, to read. The boy was not strong, and perhaps for this reason attended, aged seven, a private school in Niddry's Wynd, rather than the rowdier and more demanding High School; but the following year, presumably fitter, he did enrol at the High School. Even prior to this he was, according to his sister Barbara, fond of reading the Bible, and she told a story which indicates his impressionable nature: "One day he came running into his mother's chamber all bathed in tears, calling to her in the most earnest manner imaginable to whip him. The good woman alarmed at this unusual behaviour of her boy, enquired the cause, when he told her with all the simplicity of innocence, 'O mother! he that spareth the rod, hateth his child.'"[2]

Robert had four years at the High School, although his attendance was intermittent due to recurring ill health. Elementary Latin was the staple educational diet, and he would have gone on to read Virgil, Horace, Sallust and Livy. But when he was eleven, he was awarded (probably thanks to an approach by his mother's elder brother John Forbes, who was by now a well-to-do farmer and factor to various landowners around Old Meldrum) a "mortification" or bursary which would take him away from Edinburgh. This bursary had been instituted in 1695 by David Fergusson, a minister of Angus, for the maintenance and education of two poor children bearing the Fergusson surname, at the Grammar School of Dundee. If Robert made good progress, at the age of fourteen the bursary could be extended for four years at the University of St Andrews.

The family's financial situation also improved. In 1763 William Fergusson became managing clerk in the linen department of the British Linen Company (soon to become exclusively a bank, the British Linen Bank) in the Canongate. Meanwhile Robert's brother Hary had been apprenticed to a trade, and in 1764 Barbara married. Within a couple of years the family would leave Cap-and-Feather Close and set up house in Warriston's Close, opposite St Giles.

Dundee Grammar School had at least as good a reputation as the High School of Edinburgh, with a seven-year curriculum (although Fergusson, arriving at eleven, would be there for only two years). Almost nothing is known of his time at Dundee, but in due course he applied to the trustees of the Fergusson bursary to continue his studies at St Andrews, and in December 1764 his application was approved.

Shortly before this, in August, Robert and his mother travelled, mostly on foot, to his uncle John Forbes's farm at Roundlichnot, near Old Meldrum. They spent the month there, and a letter sent by William to his wife reminds us that the thirteen-year-old boy was still not considered very strong: "It gives me no small satisfaction to find you have had so agreeable a meeting with your brother and sisters, and that Rob has held out the journey."[3] The next time Robert went to Old Meldrum, the visit would not end so happily.

St Andrews

On 9th December 1764, Robert took up residence at Scotland's oldest university. St Andrews had then a population of about 2,000, but in most respects the town had seen better days. Fergusson's editor and biographer Alexander Grosart describes it as a "sleepy and sordid" place in which "only ale-houses abounded".[4] Thomas Pennant, visiting in 1772, would deplore the fact that "the manufactures this city might in former times possess, are now reduced to one, that of golf balls; which, trifling as it may seem, maintains several people. The trade is commonly fatal to the artists, for the balls are made by stuffing a great quantity of feathers into a leather case, by help of an iron rod, with a wooden handle, pressed against the breast, which seldom fails to bring on a consumption."[5] The town had long ceased to be the centre of Scottish ecclesiastical life, and its university had no great reputation. Attended by barely a hundred students, it was expensive (for non-bursars) and both materially and intellectually crumbling. After his visit in 1773 Dr Samuel Johnson would lament its condition: "Had the university been destroyed two centuries ago, we would not have regretted it; but to see it pining in decay and struggling for life, fills the mind with mournful images and ineffectual wishes."[6]

The most prestigious name on the academic staff was that of William Wilkie, Professor of Natural Philosophy, but, even though his poems such as the *Epigoniad* (1768) had led David Hume to describe him as "the Scottish Homer", Wilkie's reputation hardly compared with that of Hume, Adam Smith in Glasgow or the various intellectual heavyweights of

Edinburgh University. However, his eccentricity, his kindness and his literary interests (apart from his Homeric efforts he wrote animal fables, the best of which, 'The Hare and the Partan', is in Scots) together made him a kind of mentor to the young Fergusson.

Greek, Latin, Mathematics, Logic, Moral Philosophy and Natural Philosophy were all part of the curriculum. Robert seems to have excelled at mathematics, and been at least competent in the classics, although "Virgil and Horace were the only Latin authors he would ever look at while he was at the University", the younger Thomas Ruddiman reported.[7] College life for bursars was austere – they received poorer food and had to perform more duties than their fee-paying fellow students, although they were compensated with "an extremely generous daily and nightly allowance of ale"[8] – but Fergusson prospered in at least one department: he had a gift for writing witty verse. His friend Thomas Sommers later claimed that "at this time his poetical talents were beginning to appear... Every day produced something new, the offspring of his fertile pen, which was frequently employed in satyrizing the foibles of the professors, and of his fellow students".[9] "Every day" may be an exaggeration, and only one of these pieces survives, but it certainly gives an indication of his precocious ability.

The 'Elegy, on the Death of Mr David Gregory, late Professor of Mathematics in the University of St Andrews' was probably composed in the spring of 1765, just after Gregory's death and when Fergusson was only fourteen. Fergusson reworked an established form, the mock-heroic elegy using the "Standard Habbie" stanza (so named by Allan Ramsay when he adopted it from Robert Sempill's 'The Life and Death of the Piper of Kilbarchan, or the Epitaph of Habbie Simson'), but by applying it to a "respectable" subject, rather than to a piper, greyhound, horse or innkeeper, he was doing something new. There is, one feels, genuine respect (from a poet who had never been taught by the Professor) in his catalogue of Gregory's skills in algebra and architecture, and even warmth in noting his "eident care" and efforts at breaking up games of football, but every item of praise is balanced by the reductive and thumping refrain, "But now he's deid". If this early effort proved nothing else, it showed that Fergusson had a natural ability to use Scots creatively, to exploit both its comic potential and its economy of expression, as in the line "A ganging point compos'd a line".

If Fergusson's sense of humour and enjoyment of a drink made him popular with other students (though not with all of them – graffiti scribbled in the margins of university library books of the period refer to Fergusson as a "stinking fairy" and a "snake in human form", "sprung from a dung-hill" whom God would "damn eternally"[10]), relations with the professors were sometimes less cordial. In March 1768, it was the intention of the fearsome Principal Thomas Tullidelph, the "Pauly Tam" of the 'Elegy on John Hogg', to "extrude" (that is, expel) Fergusson for his participation in a student "riot" – a doubtless high-spirited battle between the winners and losers of an essay-writing competition. More seriously, Robert had also "wantonly given up John Adamson's name to be prayed for". The story behind this second incident is worth retelling:

> He was considered the best singer at the university; of consequence, he was oftener than he inclined, requested to officiate as clerk at morning and evening prayers. In order to get quit of this drudgery, he meditated the following scheme. It is usual, according to the Scottish mode of Presbyterian worship, to mention the names of persons, who are recommended in prayer; our poet, who, as usual, was in the precenter's desk, rose up with great composure, and with an audible voice, as if reading from a paper he held in his hand, said "Remember in prayer a young man [John Adamson], (who was in the hall at the very instant) who, from the sudden effects of inebriety, there appears but small hope of recovery." This, as might be expected, threw the whole students into a sudden fit of laughter. The professors wist not what to do, and the assembly broke up, and dismissed in peals of convulsive merriment.[11]

Professor Wilkie intervened to dissuade Tullidelph from expelling Fergusson, who would be leaving the University very soon anyway. Wilkie had befriended the student, and employed him over the summer months in writing out fair copies of his lectures. Robert spent days at the Professor's farm, an experience which would later provide him with the pastoral setting for his 'Eclogue' in Wilkie's memory. Possibly Wilkie also encouraged his proposed tragedy on the death of William Wallace, of which he completed two acts (like almost all his manuscripts, since lost). For a young man of unrelenting patriotic sentiments, Wallace would have been an irresistible subject.

In May 1768, Fergusson finished his studies. He did not graduate, but this was quite common, and carried no implication of failure. He stayed on for a while to work for Wilkie, but he was also needed at home in Edinburgh. His father had died the previous year, his mother had been forced to move to cheaper lodgings in Bell's Wynd, and his brother Hary, after running up debts in a failed attempt to run a fencing-school, had joined the Navy and was currently on a warship in Orkney. Robert's options were limited. A profession such as the ministry, medicine or law would require further years of study, and even if the family's financial situation had allowed, Robert had no enthusiasm for a career in any of these. The theatre and literature were what attracted him. In the immediate term, however, what he needed was a paying job, preferably one that did not take up all his available time and so might allow him to write. The only person who was in a position to exert some influence on his behalf was his uncle John Forbes.

Early in 1769 Robert went back to the Roundlichnot farm, where he stayed for six months. Accounts vary as to what caused the final falling-out between uncle and nephew, but it is not hard to see that the artistic, unconventional and physically frail eighteen-year-old would not impress the comfortably off, hard-nosed farmer and factor. Perhaps Rob's irresolution about a career exasperated Forbes; no doubt Forbes's stuffy social conservatism offended the poet. In any case, they argued, Fergusson left the farm, and, refusing Forbes's attempt at reconciliation, walked back to Edinburgh.

He reached home in a weakened condition, having lost any chance of help from his uncle.

By September, he was well enough to take up a post as clerk and copyist in the Commissary Records Office. He was offered this work by the Deputy Commissary Clerk, Charles Abercrombie, whose father had been minister of Tarland in Aberdeenshire, William Fergusson's native parish. The Commissary Office was the clerical arm of the Commissary Courts, and registered all deeds and bonds in the Lothians relating to marriage, divorce, legitimacy and wills. Fergusson's task was to transcribe these dry and repetitive documents, at a rate of pay of about a penny per page.

Much has been made by some of Fergusson's biographers of the tedium of this clerical work, and that it must have driven an imagination like his to distraction. Certainly it was dull and poorly rewarded, but he was only just nineteen, it was his first job, and he had no reason to believe he would be doing it for the rest of his working life. As it turned out, that would indeed be the case, but how was he to know this in 1769? The position gave him an income, easing the pressure on his mother (who had taken in lodgers), it was not taxing either physically or mentally, the hours allowed a full social life, and he still had time left to make excursions into the countryside and to write poetry. Furthermore, the Commissary Office was situated in Parliament Close, at Edinburgh's legal, commercial and social heart. His employment may have been, as Grosart observes, "miserably inferior to Fergusson's abilities and culture",[12] but, for someone who wrote so much from observation of the characters and events around him, it could not have been better located.

Edinburgh

For hundreds of years Edinburgh had been by far the most populous and the busiest of Scottish towns, and in spite of the Union of Parliaments in 1707 it remained a major political, legal, commercial and educational centre. In 1755 the country was still overwhelmingly rural, but Edinburgh (including Leith) boasted a population of 53,000 (swelled by numerous temporary inhabitants from other parts), about double that of its nearest rival Glasgow. (By the end of the century the two cities would be roughly equal in size, with about 80,000 people each.) Most of Edinburgh's people were crammed into the warren of closes, wynds and "lands" which stretched from Castlehill to Holyrood. Robert Chambers wrote of it as "a picturesque, odorous, inconvenient, old-fashioned town", and described how, in spite of the drawbacks of its crowded living-quarters and dark and filthy thoroughfares, a stranger would have found it a "funny, familiar, compact, and not unlikable place":

> Gentle and semple living within the compass of a single close, or even a single stair, knew and took an interest in each other. Acquaintances might not only be formed, Pyramus-and-Thisbe fashion, through party-walls, but from window to window across alleys, narrow enough in many cases to allow of hand coming to hand, and even lip to lip. There was little elegance, but a vast amount of cheap sociality. Provokingly comical clubs, founded each upon one joke, were abundant. The ladies had tea-drinkings at the primitive hour of six, from which they cruised home under the care of a lantern-bearing, patten-shod lass; or perhaps, if a bad night, in Saunders Macalpine's sedan-chair. Every forenoon, for several hours, the only clear space which the town presented – that around the Cross – was crowded with loungers of all rank... The jostle and huddlement was extreme everywhere. Gentlemen and ladies paraded along in the stately attire of the period; tradesmen chatted in groups, often bareheaded, at their shop-doors; caddies whisked about, bearing messages, or attending to the affairs of strangers; children filled the kennel [gutter] with their noisy sports. Add to all this, corduroyed men from Gilmerton, bawling coals or yellow sand... fishwomen crying their caller haddies from Newhaven; whimsicals and idiots going along, each with his or her crowd of listeners and tormentors; sootymen with their bags; town-guardsmen with their antique Lochaber axes; water-carriers with their dripping barrels; barbers with their hair-dressing materials; and so forth –

and our stranger would have been disposed to acknowledge that, though a coarse and confused, it was a perfectly unique scene, and one which, once contemplated, was not easily to be forgotten.[13]

Out of this confusion emerged two things. The first was the cultural, intellectual, literary, scientific, architectural and artistic explosion known as the Enlightenment, a Europe-wide phenomenon which blossomed with amazing vigour in Scotland, and especially in Edinburgh. Here, the municipal framework linking town and university, the presence of an educated population able to sustain and develop intellectual discourse in the form of clubs, societies and publications, and a distinctively Scottish awareness of history and civic tradition which nurtured the earliest forms of social science, meant that figures like David Hume, William Robertson, Joseph Black, James Hutton and Adam Ferguson existed not in isolation, but as the brightest stars in an entire galaxy of thinkers. "Here I stand at what is called the Cross of Edinburgh," an English visitor famously remarked, "and can, in a few minutes, take fifty men of genius and learning by the hand."[14]

The second thing that grew from the old, cheek-by-jowl Edinburgh was a need to find more space for the city to expand, and with the construction of the North Bridge and the decision to build the New Town on neo-classical lines in the late 1760s that process was begun. Ironically, it would lead to the separation of "gentle" from "semple" citizens, and thus to the destruction of the very social structure which, arguably, had provided the atmosphere of mutual interest and interaction in which enlightened thought grew. However, it is undeniable that a degree of social demarcation already existed in what would become known as the Old Town, and that the wealthier elements only tolerated living conditions there because they had no choice.

Robert Fergusson's last years coincided with this crucial moment in Edinburgh's history. Even if he had not been a great poet, his poems would be valuable today because they show us Edinburgh life as it was shortly before the gentry decamped across the Nor' Loch. When we read his descriptions of drinking-dens and scrapes with the City Guard, it is tempting to see him as living on the wilder fringes of society. In fact, excessive drinking and eating, riotous living and even riots (the Edinburgh Mob, long a force to be reckoned with by the authorities, was at this period frequently called out to protest a plethora of causes, often under the direction of a notorious cobbler called "General" Joe Smith) were the norm. Partly because domestic arrangements tended to be so cramped, social life revolved around public meeting-places: the law-courts, the Cross, the coffee-houses, the theatre, and, above all, the taverns. The culture which Fergusson became part of in 1769, whatever else it was, was not a *salon* culture.

When the famed operatic singer Giusto Ferdinando Tenducci came to Edinburgh in the summer of 1769, Robert made his acquaintance. He was already interested in the theatre and music, and had a fine singing voice himself. At performances of Thomas Arne's opera *Artaxerxes* at the Theatre Royal in the Canongate, Tenducci introduced three new songs set to popular Scottish airs, with lyrics by "Mr R. Fergusson, Edinburgh". Not only was this Robert's debut as a public author, it was the last work performed at the theatre, which by the end of the year had been replaced by a new one in Shakespeare Square, across the North Bridge. (Fergusson would later write a burlesque poem, 'The Canongate Playhouse in Ruins'.) Tenducci left Edinburgh in November for London, but Fergusson's other friends included the actor William Woods, the city's Master of Music and principal singer at St Cecilia's Hall Cornforth Gilson, the composer John Collet, and Robert Anderson, a medical student who would later edit *British Poets*. Through such contacts he developed a passionate interest in the theatre, attending as many plays as he could. Through his friendship with Woods he was usually admitted free of charge.

Perhaps because theatre in Scotland was so dependent on trends set in London, his attempts at poetry tended in the same direction. On 7th February 1771 Walter Ruddiman's *Weekly Magazine* published "three Pastorals, under the titles of Morning, Noon and Night, written by a young gentleman of this place, the style of which appears as natural and picturesque as that of any of the modern ones hitherto published". Modelled on the work of William Shenstone, these, his first published verses, are quite forgettable. More followed, a mixture of imitative sentimental and burlesque pieces, published presumably because they fulfilled all the criteria of what constituted fashionable verse – exhibiting tasteful delicacy, polite humour and touching sentiment. This was the year in which Henry Mackenzie published *The Man of Feeling*, a novel which would take Britain and then Europe by storm, and which extolled polite sensibility as one of the highest virtues. Fergusson undoubtedly read it, as did Burns, who wore out two copies. Mackenzie, who would champion Burns as "this Heaven-taught ploughman", praising his English poems but seeing his class, education and Scots language as fatal barriers to fame and success, later passed harsh judgment on Fergusson's character, effectively blaming him for being a bad role-model for Burns. It is ironic, therefore, that Fergusson was temporarily lured by the cult of feeling epitomised by Mackenzie, and, as Grosart puts it, that he "missed seeing for the time... *the* vein that he was destined to work".[15]

However, it is a mistake to think of Fergusson as being faced with a straight choice between writing in English and writing in Scots, as if these were mutually incompatible. If the model of English poets like Shenstone, John Gay and Thomas Gray was available to him, so was the example of Allan Ramsay. Ramsay (1684–1758), originally from Lanarkshire, was a wigmaker turned bookseller, poet and editor, who settled in Edinburgh, founded the Easy Club (a political and literary debating society), opened a theatre, and articulated a fiercely Jacobite cultural nationalism while managing to avoid becoming entangled in either the 'Fifteen or the 'Forty-five. In his collections *The Ever Green* and *The Tea-Table Miscellany* he republished important Scottish texts, popularising work by the Renaissance makars William Dunbar, Robert Henryson and Gavin Douglas, as well as traditional songs and ballads and more contemporary Scots verse. He also wrote his own poetry, half of it in flowery Augustan English, half in a robust Scots. Poems such as the

'Elegy on Maggy Johnston', the 'Elegy on Lucky Wood in the Canongate' and 'Lucky Spence's Last Advice', celebrated the raucous life of Edinburgh taverns and brothels, often using the Standard Habbie stanza. His hugely popular work, *The Gentle Shepherd*, was a pastoral romance, complete with songs, which set the then fashionable idea of a rustic idyll in the countryside near Edinburgh, and utilised both a lively Scots and more formal English. Fergusson would take up most of Ramsay's ideas and develop them, and, like him, he saw no dilemma in writing in both languages. It is not surprising that, after his first four poems in Scots were published in *The Weekly Magazine*, he was addressed by an admirer in a verse epistle which began, "Is Allan risen frae the deid?"

Walter Ruddiman, the publisher of *The Weekly Magazine*, was the nephew of Thomas Ruddiman, who had published Ramsay's work. The *Magazine*, which flourished from 1768 to 1784, was a compilation of news items, essays, articles and poetry, which achieved sales in the capital and throughout Scotland of up to 3,000 an issue. When, on 2nd January 1772, Ruddiman published Fergusson's 'The Daft-Days', he was introducing a startlingly fresh voice, writing in a rich Scots that had not been seen in print since Ramsay. The paper's readers responded with delight. The 'Elegy on the Death of Scots Music', 'The King's Birth-Day in Edinburgh', 'Caller Oysters', 'Braid Claith', 'Hallow-Fair' and 'To the Tron-Kirk Bell' followed at intervals during the rest of the year. As a series, these poems provide a noisy, colourful picture of Edinburgh, focusing in particular on its street characters and taverns: they abound with tipplers and dandies; the gentry have their wigs set alight by fireworks or are flattened by flying dead cats during street parties which are more akin to riots; oysters are recommended as a cure for "plouky noses"; and citizens the worse for drink are regularly beaten up by Highland polismen. An actor friend Frederick Guion (later an acquaintance of Burns) wasted no time in referring to Fergusson as the "laureate" of the city. Such verse may not have presented the image of a sophisticated Edinburgh which some of the literati would have preferred, but Fergusson had found, simultaneously, his *métier* and his *milieu*.

It was in the taverns that Edinburgh's extraordinary club life flourished. Some clubs, such as the Select Society (which ceased in 1763) and the Speculative Society (which still survives today), existed primarily for debates and lectures among the literati on a wide range of cultural and scientific topics. Others had their origins in a single issue: the Poker Club (1762–1787), for example, was founded by Adam Ferguson and others to promote the establishment of a Scottish militia, though debating other subjects of national interest naturally followed, as did the consumption of a good dinner. Some clubs met in the afternoon, others in the evening, but most, however much drink might have been taken, strictly regulated their meetings, the commonest rule being that sessions were wound up by ten o'clock at night. Among the many 18th-century clubs noted by Chambers were the Pious Club (which met in a *pie-house*), the Spendthrift Club (members were limited to spending fourpence halfpenny per night), the Dirty Club (no gentlemen to appear in clean linen), the Black Wigs (members wore black wigs), the Odd Fellows (members wrote their names upside down), the Bonnet Lairds (members wore blue bonnets), the Mirror, the Diversorium, the Haveral, the Six Foot, the Assembly of Birds, the Humdrum, the Blast and Quaff, the Pipe, the Knights of the Cap and Feather, and the Sweating Club. This last belonged to a species which had discarded all pretensions to enlightenment. Chambers records:

> After intoxicating themselves, it was their custom to sally forth at midnight, and attack whomsoever they met upon the streets. Any luckless wight who happened to fall into their hands was chased, jostled, pinched, and pulled about, till he not only perspired, but was ready to drop down and die with exhaustion. Even so late as the early years of this [the 19th] century, it was unsafe to walk the streets of Edinburgh at night on account of the numerous drunken parties of young men who then reeled about, bent on mischief, at all hours, and from whom the Town-guard were unable to protect the sober citizen.[16]

The club of which Robert Fergusson became a member on 10th October 1772, the Cape, was more highbrow than this, but it never had the intellectual or social status of, say, the Poker Club. Although there were members who were printers, painters, musicians and literary antiquaries, more were respectable tradesmen. As the club's surviving papers make clear, conviviality was an essential part of the Cape's *raison d'être*:

> After the business of the day was over to pass the evening socially with a set of select companions in an agreeable, but at the same time a rational and frugal manner; for this purpose beer and porter were the usual liquors, from fourpence to sixpence each the extent of their usual expense; conversation and a song their amusement, gaming generally prohibited; and a freedom to come and go at their pleasure was always considered essential to the constitution of the Society.[17]

The Cape was non-exclusive and unpretentious. Between 1764 and 1800 some 650 candidates for membership were admitted. Fergusson was the 159th, but regular attendance was kept up by only a hard core, to which he definitely belonged for the next year or so. Among the better known names which gave the club its Bohemian reputation over the years, may be mentioned David Herd, the collector and editor of *Ancient and Modern Scottish Songs*, the painters Alexander Runciman, Alexander Nasmyth, Jacob Moir and Henry Raeburn, and the housebreaker Deacon William Brodie.

Meetings took place in one or other tavern, usually Walter Scott's in Geddes Close, and the venue was designated Cape Hall for the duration. There were various dignitaries appointed, such as a Sovereign, a Hereditary Chaplain, Councillors, a Recorder, Treasurer and Secretary. Ordinary members were known as Knights Companions of the Cape, and novices were introduced through a solemn ceremony which involved the taking of an oath of fealty and being "knighted" with a poker, at which time the club motto, "C.F.D." (standing for *Concordia Fratrum Decus*, or "Harmony among Brothers is a Fine Thing") was pronounced by the Sovereign. The knight elect then had to recount some adventure from his past, and from it the Sovereign extracted a suitable title by which he would henceforth be known. Fergusson, presumably having told of his near-expulsion from St Andrews, was dubbed "Sir Precenter". Other members went by such exotic handles as Sir Partan, Sir Nun and Abbess, Sir Hayloft, Sir Beefsteaks, Sir Old Wife, Sir Baboon, Sir Marriage, Sir Tumult and Sir Macaroni.

As Matthew P. McDiarmid has pointed out, "so excellent a constitution and such proper pomp and circumstance might easily lead us to forget that all this time we are still in a tavern".[18] McDiarmid quotes from the club records an incident of "High Jinks" which gives a flavour of what Cape members could get up to in the small hours, and there is no doubt that the combination of mock-chivalry, sustained drinking, song and conversation suited Fergusson's personality perfectly. He wrote lines lampooning the members, and contributed to *The Capeiad*, a miscellany of bawdy songs, jokes and drinking ditties. A few stanzas of his parody of 'The Broom of Cowdenknowes', under the title 'A Mournful Ditty from the Knight of Complaints', give the flavour:

> How blyth was I ilk day to see
>   Auchleck come tripping doun
> His ain forestairs at Netherbow
>   To drink his dram at Noon
>
> *Chorus*
> Oh the Shades the Caller Caller Shades
>   Where I have oft complaind
> Till Luckies Bottle C.F.D.
>   Was to the bottom drain'd
>
> I neither wanted drink nor dram
>   Whan Tam Dicks house was nigh
> But now in Canongate I dwell
>   A dismal place and dry
>
> Hard fate that I should banish'd be
>   Gang heavily and mourn
> Because I lood the Warmest dram
>   That Eer in Mouth did burn...

> Adiew ye Cooling Shades adiew
>   Fareweel my forenoons Gill
> By Tam Dicks fire I'll Sitt no more
>   My Horrors all to kill[19]

A sketch of Fergusson reading to the Cape Club, probably by Alexander Runciman, who was a close friend, exists in the National Library of Scotland. It shows a thin, lank-haired and frail-looking young man. We also have the following description from Thomas Sommers:

> He was in person about five feet, six inches high, and well shaped. His complexion fair, but rather pale. His eyes full, black, and piercing. His nose long, his lips thin, his teeth well set and white. His neck long, and well proportioned. His shoulders narrow, and his limbs long, but more sinewy than fleshy. His voice, strong, clear, and melodious. Remarkably fond of old Scots songs, and the *best* singer of the *Birks of Invermay* I ever heard. When speaking, he was quick, forcible, and complaisant. In walking, he appeared smart, erect, and unaffected.[20]

From Sommers we also get a story that illuminates Fergusson's sheer *joie de vivre* at this time:

> Such were his vocal powers, and attachment to *Scots* songs, that in the course of his convivial frolics, he laid a wager with some of his associates, that if they would furnish him with a certain number of printed ballads, (no matter of what kind), he would undertake to dispose of them as a *street* singer in the course of two hours. The bet was laid; and next evening, being in the month of November, a large bundle of ballads was procured for him. He wrapped himself in a shabby great coat, put on an old scratch wig, and in this disguised form, commenced his adventure at the weigh house, head of the West Bow. In his going down the Lawnmarket, and High Street, he had the address to collect great multitudes around him, while he amused them with a variety of favourite Scots songs, by no means such as he had ballads for, and gained the wager, by disposing of the whole collection. He waited

on his companions by eight o'clock that evening, and spent with them in mirthful glee, the produce of his street adventure.[21]

On another occasion, according to Sommers, the poet threw a stone with a canting grace attached into a meeting of the Glassites, a strict non-conforming sect; and on another, he disguised himself as a sailor and "sallying out, paid a round of visits to his acquaintances":

> He was so effectually disguised that few or none of them knew him, and by throwing forth hints of some of their former indiscretions, he so much surprised them, that they imputed his knowledge to divination. By this means he procured from many of them such a fund of information, as enabled him to give them a greater surprise when he resumed the genuine character of Robby Fergusson. For in the sailor's habit he informed them of many frailties and failings which they imagined it impossible for any one of his appearance to know; and in the habit of Robby Fergusson, he divulged many things which they believed none but the ragged sailor was acquainted with.[22]

On one subject there is a strange silence, or at least absence of information: Fergusson's love life, if he had one. Matthew P. McDiarmid uncovered a brief relationship, conducted partly through pastoral verses, between Fergusson and a married woman, also a poet, around 1771-2, but it is impossible now to tell whether it was more than an exercise in stylised romance. Fergusson was "Damon" to her "Stella" (one thinks, inevitably, of Burns's "Sylvander" and Agnes McLehose's "Clarinda"), and after his death she wrote to *The Weekly Magazine* of his "raging love" for her, feelings which her circumstances meant she could return only as sympathetic friendship.[23] There is, apart from his version of 'The Lee-Rigg', a total absence of love interest in his poetry: his most affectionate lines are addressed to his male friends. His many biographers say almost nothing on this aspect of his life. Either there was nothing to be said; or, like many men at the time, he had relations with prostitutes, which could not be mentioned; or, possibly, he was homosexual. Edwin Morgan has discussed this,[24] and it is certainly interesting to speculate whether Fergusson's sexuality had anything to do with his later depression. But, at a distance of some 250 years, we will never really know.

By the end of 1772 Fergusson had written enough to consider putting together a book of poems. He was also planning to translate Virgil's *Eclogues* and *Georgics*, and publish them with a new edition of Gavin Douglas's translation of the *Aeneid*, although this scheme was never realised. But Walter Ruddiman was prepared to publish a collection of Fergusson's poems by subscription, and this duly appeared in January 1773. It sold some 500 copies and made Fergusson £50 – not a bad sum, but the sales were probably disappointing after the enthusiastic response to his work in *The Weekly Magazine*. Perhaps the balance of poems (twenty-seven in English, nine in Scots) was a misjudgment. At any rate, enough copies still remained in 1779, when the remainder of his poems were published, to call the second volume "Part II" and sell them together as a set. Ruddiman, however, remained a faithful patron. He published Fergusson fortnightly and even weekly throughout 1773, paying him regularly for his work. Previously, he had even provided him with two suits of clothes, which may have been a friendly criticism on Fergusson's usual dishevelled and shabby appearance.

Meanwhile Fergusson had been working on another ambitious project, a long poem in Scots, intended to stretch to several cantos, on Edinburgh itself. Early in 1773, he published its opening 328-line canto himself, under the title *Auld Reikie, A Poem*. It was not republished till 1779, when a further forty lines were added, but this is all that survives of a grandiose scheme. 'Auld Reikie' is an unfinished masterpiece, occupying a place in Fergusson's opus akin to *Weir of Hermiston* in Stevenson's. Scene by scene, from dawn to night, the city is portrayed, its sights, smells and sounds captured in fine detail: there is criticism of civic policy and despair over the blighted lives of some inhabitants, but the overwhelming sense, summarised in its final lines of homesick thoughts from Fife, is of deep affection.

The satirical note struck in parts of 'Auld Reikie' continued in poems like 'Mutual Complaint of Plainstanes and Causey', 'The Rising of the Session', 'The Ghaists' and 'On Seeing a Butterfly in the Street'. It was also to be found in 'The Sow of Feeling', published in *The Weekly Magazine* in April. A response to Henry Mackenzie's latest work, *The Prince of Tunis* – an overwrought melodrama performed at the theatre to general applause – Fergusson's poem recasts the Man of Feeling as a sensitive sow, lamenting the slaughter of her husband and children:

> Thrice happy, had I liv'd in Jewish time,
> When swallowing pork or pig was doom'd a crime;
> My husband long had blest my longing arms,
> Long, long had known love's sympathetic charms!

The poem also takes a sideswipe at pastoralism, as the sow recalls better days in a "verdant grove":

> 'Twas there I listen'd to his warmest vows,
> Amidst the pendant melancholy boughs;
> 'Twas there my trusty lover shook for me
> A show'r of acorns from the oaken tree;
> And from the teeming earth, with joy, plough'd out
> The roots salubrious with his hardy snout.

'The Sow of Feeling' hardly bears comparison with Fergusson's Scots poems, but it shows him asserting his independence and happily undermining literary fashion, and probably did little to endear him to Mackenzie. He had come a long way in only two years.

His own attachment to the countryside manifested itself in several poems over the spring and summer of 1773. He had already written two 'Eclogues', one in memory of Professor Wilkie, the other in which two shepherds, Sandie and Willie, discuss how Sandie's marriage is in a rocky state due to his wife's devotion to tea. In April he published the reflective 'Ode to the Bee', written from Broomhouse in East Lothian;

in May appeared the sublime 'Farmer's Ingle', a fond but not over-sentimental hymn to rural life; in July came 'Hame Content' and in August 'Ode to the Gowdspink'. The latter poem was addressed from North Belton, East Lothian. This was the estate of his friend James Hay, and he stayed here for most of August, keeping company with another companion, Charles Lorimer. Lorimer was about the same age as Fergusson, but since 1771 had been Collector in the Customs at Dunbar. It was from Dunbar, and probably through Lorimer's arrangement, that an expedition to the Isle of May and on to Fife was organised. Fergusson was less than complimentary about Fife in the poem he published in *The Weekly Magazine* describing this voyage, and was apparently challenged to a duel by an offended Dunfermline man. He declined to accept. The following month he attacked his old university, for having "treated" Samuel Johnson with foreign fare when they should (according to his poem) have subjected the notoriously Scotophobic doctor to a meal of "gudely hameil gear". To be rude about St Andrews and Johnson in the same poem shows how self-assured he had become.

Near the end of September Fergusson accompanied his friend James Wilson, a naval officer, to visit an old companion, Charles Salmon, who had left Walter Ruddiman's business to work for a printer in Dumfries. Fergusson's poem 'Dumfries' duly appeared in that town's own *Weekly Magazine* on the 28th. About this time he must have learned of the death at Newcastle of John Cunningham, a poet whom he admired. Fergusson composed and published as a tract a poem to his memory written in Cunningham's own Shenstone-influenced style. It has not stood the test of time, and indeed its chief interest now is that it presaged Fergusson's own deterioration: Cunningham had died in the madhouse, and his fate seems to have affected his fellow-poet badly. A few more poems appeared in the last three months of 1773, including 'The Sitting of the Session', 'A Drink Eclogue' and 'To My Auld Breeks'. Though all exhibit some of the qualities of Fergusson's best work, there is a slight weariness or sombreness about them. 'To My Auld Breeks' is a particularly moving mixture of comedy and, as in these lines, valediction:

> You've seen me round the bickers reel
> Wi heart as hale as temper'd steel,
> And face sae apen, free and blyth,
> Nor thought that sorrow there could kyth;
> But the neist mament this was lost,
> Like gowan in December's frost.

Apart from the half-humorous, half-pathetic 'Last Will' and its 'Codicile', and possibly a few grim pieces such as the 'Ode to Horror' and 'On Night', Rob Fergusson's engagement with the muse was over.

Decline and Fall

In October 1773 he wrote in a letter to a friend: "The town is dull at present; I am thoroughly idle, and that fancy which has so often afforded me pleasure, almost denies to operate but on the gloomiest subjects". He signed the letter, "Your afflicted humble servant".[25] He worked on at the Commissary Office until the end of the year, but did not return after the New Year holidays.

What brought about this seemingly sudden change of mood? A careful reading of the poems shows, in fact, that Fergusson had often been inclined to sombre contemplation even when at his most ebullient. Not far from the barefoot housemaids and stairhead critics of 'Auld Reikie' stands the prostitute "wi heavy een and sour grimace"; and the cheerful, healthy Knights of the Cape are contrasted with the group "sae dismal, dim, / Wi horrid aspect, cleeding dim" that Death has claimed for his "dowy crew". But such a mix of emotions and thoughts is hardly unnatural. In late 1773, though, the balance shifted, dramatically and permanently.

Some early biographers sought to make a moral lesson out of Fergusson, painting his last days as being full of remorse for his previous debauched existence. This would explain his renewed interest in Christianity, his burning of all his manuscripts, and his statement, "I am satisfied – I feel some consolation in never having written anything against religion."²⁶ Others put his collapse down to a combination of unfortunate social background and alcohol addiction. Certainly this theory enabled Henry Mackenzie to draw some sanctimonious conclusions about the three giants of 18th-century Scots poetry:

> Fergus[s]on, dissipated and drunken, died in early life, after having produced poems faithfully and humorously describing scenes of Edinburgh of festivity and somewhat of blackguardism...
>
> Burns, originally virtuous, was seduced by dissipated companions, and after he got into the Excise addicted himself to drunkenness, tho' the rays of his genius sometimes broke through the mist of his dissipation... His great admiration of Fergus[s]on shewed his propensity to coarse dissipation.

Allan Ramsay, on the other hand, "having by his good conduct and liveliness got into very respectable society... lived happily and died leaving a family well enough provided for".²⁷ A more sympathetic writer to both Burns and Fergusson, Alexander Peterkin, who defended both against character assassins, published an edition of the latter's work in 1807. He had been informed, by an anonymous but credible witness, that the poet had contracted syphilis. The symptoms of this disease might tie in with the depression, anxiety and restlessness from which he suffered, or knowing that he had syphilis might simply have encouraged a tendency to depression already present: in either case, this story is not corroborated by others. According to Peterkin's witness, while receiving medical treatment, Fergusson was persuaded to go to Fife with some gentlemen on electioneering business, and was there "much exposed to the riotous enjoyments incident to such occasions; and these, in conjunction with his disordered health, produced a feverishness and decrepitude of mind amounting nearly to insanity". By March 1774 he was "very poorly", and "quite aware that his mind was in disorder, and he anticipated with terror, the confinement in a mad-house, which he saw would be unavoidable".²⁸

Small wonder that he descended into religious gloom. A brief stay outwith the city at Restalrig did not relieve his depression, and he went back to his mother's. Past conversations with more than one minister on the mortality of the flesh and the coming judgment now returned to haunt him; the noise of a cat catching and killing a starling that had come down the chimney set his nerves further on edge; he turned more and more to the Bible and became increasingly isolated.

Meanwhile letters to *The Weekly Magazine* were asking what had become of its "agreeable poet". At a meeting of the Cape on 2nd July it was unanimously agreed to raise a collection, both from existing club funds and from individual members, to assist a young gentleman "who has been a considerable time past in distress". It even appeared that about this time Fergusson was making some kind of progress, as his friend William Woods published some lines 'To Mr R. Fergusson: On his Recovery' in *The Caledonian Mercury* of 9th July. But less than three weeks later the same paper was announcing that the poet had been "seiz'd with a very dangerous illness". According to Thomas Sommers:

> ... he was one evening taking a glass with a few friends, and had the misfortune to fall from a stair-case, by which he received a violent contusion on the head. Upon being carried home to his mother's house, he could give no account by what means he met with the accident, being in a state of total insensibility. His brain being disordered, he became so furious, that three men could hardly restrain his violence. From the distress into which his poor mother was plunged and her inability to render him necessary attendance in her own house, she was obliged to remove him to the public asylum. But in order to effect this removal, it was found necessary to practise a deception, which was accomplished by a few of his most intimate acquaintances. On pretence of asking him in the evening to visit a friend, they put him into a sedan chair, and conducted him to a cell of that dreary and sequestered mansion. He soon discovered his confined situation, and in frantic rage, accompanied with hideous shouts, assailed the ears, and

roused the shrieks of the other wretched captives in the house, while his companions "stood speechless, fixed in all the death of woe"; and felt on their minds an impression too strong ever to be removed.[29]

Prior to this last resort being taken, Fergusson had been attended at home by a young doctor from the University. Andrew Duncan (1744–1828) had studied medicine at St Andrews, but now worked in Edinburgh, where he would become a professor in 1790. His notes corroborate the desperate state Fergusson was in as described by Sommers. Duncan continued to visit Fergusson in the Bedlam, and it was his case which first spurred him to campaign for better treatment and conditions for the mentally ill. "It is impossible", he later wrote, "to conceive a more interesting object of Charity than the Man of Genius when a Pauper Lunatic."[30] In 1813 Duncan established a new mental hospital in Morningside, a vast improvement on the terrible place where the poet languished.

Fergusson spent two months in the Bedlam, sometimes exclaiming that he "should be a minister of the glorious gospel", at others singing "with a beauty and pathos and tremulous tenderness the 'Birks of Invermay' and other favourite Scottish melodies, such as before he had never reached".[31] Sommers visited the poet a few days before his death, accompanied by Dr John Aitken, another medical reformer:

> We got immediate access to the cell, and found Robert lying with his clothes on, stretched upon a bed of loose uncovered straw. The moment he heard my voice, he instantly arose – got me in his arms and wept! The Doctor felt his pulse, and declared it to be favourable. I asked the keeper (whom I formerly knew as a gardener) to allow him to accompany us into an adjoining back court, by way of taking the air. He consented. Robert took hold of me by the arm, placing me on his right, and the doctor on his left, and in this form we walked back and forth along the court, conversing for nearly an hour...

> Having passed about two hours with him on this visit, we found it necessary to take our leave, the doctor assuring him, that he would soon be restored to his friends, and that I would visit him again in a day or two... Neither of us, however, had an opportunity of accomplishing our promise; for in a few days thereafter, I received an intimation from the keeper that Robert Fergusson had breathed his last, without the smallest symptom of pain![32]

Robert Fergusson died on 17th October 1774, having reached his twenty-fourth birthday six weeks before. "Mr Ferguson, in the Cels" was the perfunctory item in the Bedlam minute book next day. He was buried two days later in the Canongate Kirkyard, in an unmarked grave. Ironically, a few days earlier his brother Hary, now overseas, had sent a remittance to his mother, and she had hoped to bring Robert home to look after him herself. And shortly after his death she received a letter from a former friend of Robert in India, informing her that he had procured a handsome position for him, and that she should equip him for the voyage and send him out immediately. With the letter was a draft of £100 to cover expenses.

Legacy and Influence

Fergusson lived at a time when the question of Scottish identity – political, cultural, linguistic – was, even when not explicitly debated, very much in people's minds. The Union of Parliaments was not half a century old, and deeply resented by many, when he was born; there had been several minor and two major Jacobite risings, during the last of which, in 1745, Edinburgh had been occupied by Prince Charles Edward's army. On the other hand social and literary trends increasingly inclined towards closer integration and assimilation with England, especially with London. This was the era of "North Britain" (a coinage which was not reciprocated by the inhabitants of South Britain), when Boswell desperately ingratiated himself with Dr Johnson, giant intellects such as David Hume anxiously sought to expunge Scotticisms from their writings, and the aspiring middle and upper classes took elocution lessons from Irish actors and studied, in order to avoid them, lists of phrases "liable to be mistaken for English in this country". James Beattie, a native of Laurencekirk in Kincardineshire, produced perhaps the most comprehensive of these, *Scotticisms, Arranged in Alphabetical Order, Designed to Correct Improprieties of Speech and Writing*, in 1779. This helpful volume warned Scots that, even if they could train their tongues to say "bread" instead of "breid", there was a further gaffe to be avoided, in that they should refer to "a bit *of* bread" not "a bit bread". Using "stay" for "live", "to my bed" for "to bed" and "he has got the cold" for "he has got a cold", were other dangerous traps for unwary Scots.[33] Specifically Scots words, such as "eident", "skelp" and "braw" (to take three examples from the first poem in this book), were of course to be dropped completely.

The situation was more complex than this, though. Beattie, who was Professor of Moral Philosophy at Aberdeen for three decades from 1760, and who attacked Hume's scepticism, was also a poet, and occasionally wrote in a nostalgic, rural Scots. Some leading establishment figures, especially in the legal profession, disdained to speak in English, while among the lower classes, in town and country, it was, if spoken at all, reserved for very formal occasions and reading the Bible. Ambitious men who retained a sense of Scottish pride were torn between wishing to express themselves "correctly" and not wishing to see the "old Scots words" disappear entirely. Orthography was a further problem: "bread" could equally serve to represent both Scots and English pronunciations, as could "night", "town" and "pleasure"; but as English became dominant, readers would increasingly fail to recognise the Scots alternative. Allan Ramsay had tried to remind his fellow Scots of the literary glories of the makars, yet apart from himself few attempted to write a sustained poetry, let alone prose, in Scots. At this juncture, establishing a pattern which has been repeated right down to the present, people began to grieve over the dying Scots language, which, they declared, would soon, probably within a generation, be utterly extinct.

Fergusson, as we have seen, was not immune to such contradictions and complications. They extended far beyond language in any case. In 'The Daft-Days' and 'Elegy, on the Death of Scots Music', for example, he appears to mount a sturdy defence of all things Scottish against "vile Italian tricks" – yet this was the man who counted Tenducci as a friend, who named William Macgibbon, a composer who specialised in Italianate style, as his champion, and who adored the theatre with all *its* foreign influences. What Fergusson did, however, was to take new ideas and graft them onto a native plant which he was determined not just to preserve but to make flourish.

His family origins in the North-East, his close association with the Ruddimans, who were Jacobites and Episcopalians also from that part of Scotland, his education and his own intense Tory patriotism, meant that he was heir to a tradition of Scottish Humanism which made a virtue of rural tradition as opposed to urban mercantilism, and which was deeply suspicious of both Whig politics and Whig (that is, Presbyterian) religious orthodoxy. Preservation of Scots language and stanzaic forms, combined with classical allusions and models such as the eclogue, ode and pastoral, also point to Fergusson's awareness of this Humanist legacy, though how consciously he built it into his poems is debatable.[34] What is certainly true is that his own exuberant personality generally overruled the kind of stultifying nostalgia that was already accreting to romantic Jacobitism.

His use of Scots – not a thin, backward-looking or narrow-grounded Scots but a language which was rich, contemporary and able to address a wide range of subjects – is all the more refreshing when seen against this background. He had several advantages: a knowledge and experience of different dialects, from Aberdeenshire through Fife and Edinburgh to East Lothian, so that, like almost every successful poet in Scots before and since, he wrote in an amalgamated *literary* language, not a regional dialect; a thorough grounding in the speech of Edinburgh, which naturally he spoke himself; and – something which neither Ramsay nor Burns had – a college education, which gave him access to the classics, as well as an early familiarity with Scottish and English literature. There is a confidence about his work which comes only partly from his undoubted precocity and self-belief: his education was also responsible. It enabled him, for example, to draw in figures from classical literature and domesticate them almost as hamely Edinburgh citizens, and to drop in Latin phrases with unaffected ease – skills which were unavailable to Burns. The same confidence is seen in the last two stanzas of 'Braid Claith', where he gets away with rhyming "snout on" with "Newton" in the course of passing some astute comments about dress-sense. Here is a poet entirely at ease with his subject-matter, his allusions to famous men and educational attainments, and his verse-form:

> Braid Claith gies fock an unco heeze;
> Makes mony kail-worms butter-flies;
> Gies mony a doctor his degrees
>   For little skaith;
> In short, you may be what you please
>   Wi gude Braid Claith.
>
> For thof ye had as wise a snout on
> As Shakespeare or Sir Isaac Newton,
> Your judgment fouk would hae a dout on
>   I'll tak my aith,
> Till they could see you wi a suit on
>   O' gude Braid Claith.

Fergusson took the Standard Habbie and, without excluding comedy, raised that stanza-form to a status where it could treat a range of emotions, moods and ideas. In the final verse of 'The Sitting of the Session', we see that economical mix of profundity and homeliness which Burns would develop with still greater success:

> But law's a draw-well unco deep,
> Withouten rim fock out to keep:
> A donnart chiel, whan drunk, may dreep
>   Fu sleely in,
> But finds the gate baith stey and steep
>   Ere out he win.

The same acknowledgement of a proverb-rich folk tradition appears in 'The Farmer's Ingle', in lines like "Sair wark and poortith downa weel be join'd" and "The mind's ay cradled when the grave is near"; or again, in the final couplet of 'On Seeing a Butterfly in the Street':

> And may they scad their lips fu leal,
> That dip their spoons in ither's kail.

In poems like 'Hallow-Fair' and 'The Election' he turned to the stanza-form of old poems such as 'Peblis to the Play' and 'Christ's Kirk on the Green', which had been reprinted by Ramsay, and injected them with a wit and sharpness of observation which removes any sense of mere imitation. The same is true of the 'Eclogues' and dialogue poems like the 'Mutual Complaint of Plainstanes and Causey' and 'The Ghaists', poems which address topical and quite local issues but which, through his characterisation and linguistic dexterity, still speak to us today. In these and other poems, too, Fergusson's use of irony is more sophisticated than it appears in his satires in English, such as 'The Sow of Feeling'. The pavement and the street arguing about their heavy loads are like two old men seeking to outdo each other's grievances, but Plainstanes (a very subtle parody of the Man of Feeling) confesses that it is more thrilling to be stepped on by some feet than by others:

> I grant, indeed, that, now and than,
> Yield to a *paten's* pith I maun;
> But patens, tho' they're aften plenty,
> Are aye laid down wi feet fou tenty,
> And stroaks frae ladies, tho' they're teazing,
> I freely maun avow are pleasing.

A similar argument rages between Brandy and Whisky in 'A Drink Eclogue', when each bottle accuses the other of causing greater social distress, while painting himself as a benefactor. The "Frenchman", having puffed up his own court connections and poured disdain on the Highland antecedents and low taste of the "haveril Scot", appeals to the Landlady's judgment in deciding which is the better drink. It turns out that she has been plagued with so much tax that she has resorted to passing off whisky dyed with saffron as brandy. Brandy and Whisky are thus revealed as one and the same, giving an added hypocritical slant to the former's pretensions. The Landlady concludes:

> Will you your breeding threep, ye mongrel loun!
> Frae hame-bred liquor dy'd to colour broun?
> So flunky braw, whan drest in master's claes,
> Struts to Auld Reikie's cross on sunny days,
> Till some auld comrade, ablins out o' place,
> Near the vain upstart shaws his meagre face;
> Bumbaz'd he loups frae sight, and jooks his ken,
> Fley'd to be seen amang the tassel'd train.

In 'The Farmer's Ingle' Fergusson produced something quite new in Scottish writing, and here the influence of Shenstone was beneficial. He took the Spencerian stanza from Shenstone, but while retaining the same rhyming scheme made all nine lines iambic pentameters, and only used an alexandrine line of six feet at the end of three of the stanzas. The effect of this in the last stanza, as David Daiches has pointed out, is "a beautifully modulated ending", "an organ-noted benediction" to an affectionate but realistic poem depicting country life:

> May Scotia's simmers ay look gay and green,
>   Her yellow har'sts frae scowry blasts decreed;
> May a' her tenants sit fu snug and bien,
>   Frae the hard grip of ails and poortith freed,
>   And a lang lasting train o' peaceful hours succeed.

"Except for 'lang' and perhaps 'o'' this line could take its place easily in an English poem," Daiches writes. "But it is a tribute to Fergusson's mastery of his medium that it takes its place with equal ease in a poem written in Scots. For though 'The Farmer's Ingle' is a Scots poem, this does not mean that it derives entirely and solely from Scottish literary tradition. On the contrary, the stanza form, the tone and even the subject show English influence; the significant point is that these influences have been thoroughly assimilated, and are used in an assured Scots way."[35] Such assimilation is not characteristic of a literature lacking in confidence. Perhaps more than anything, Fergusson gave Scots poetry renewed self-belief at a vital moment.

As proof, we have Burns's own testimony, in his letter of 2nd August 1787 to Dr Moore: "Rhyme, except some religious pieces which are in print, I had given up; but meeting with Fergusson's Scotch Poems, I strung anew my wildly-sounding rustic lyre with emulating vigour." This, as Matthew P. McDiarmid has convincingly argued, refers probably to the year 1784.[36] It was from that year, till 1786, that the creative power in Burns was unleashed which resulted in his Kilmarnock edition. In April 1785 he referred to "Fergusson the bauld and slee" in the 'First Epistle to J. Lapraik', and in May he raged to William Simpson of Ochiltree against Edinburgh's neglect of its poet:

> O Fergusson! thy glorious parts
> Ill-suited law's dry, musty arts!
> My curse upon your whunstane hearts
>   Ye E'nbrugh Gentry!
> The tythe o' what ye waste at cartes
>   Wad stow'd his pantry!

In August in his Commonplace Book he wrote of "the excellent Ramsay, and the still more excellent Fergusson". Clearly something in the dead city poet's work triggered a response in the Ayrshire farmer. It has been pointed out that Fergusson, at twenty-three, had written far more poetry in Scots than had Burns at the same age. But after reading Fergusson, the flow from Burns's pen turned into a flood.

The debt owed by Burns, so often acknowledged by himself, has been well documented, and is clearly evident in poems such as 'The Cotter's Saturday Night' (to 'The Farmer's Ingle'), 'The Brigs of Ayr' (to 'Mutual Complaint of Plainstanes and Causey'), 'The Holy Fair' and 'Halloween' (to 'Hallow-Fair' and 'Leith Races'), 'The Ordination' (to 'The Election'), 'To a Haggis' (to 'Caller Oysters'), 'To a Mountain Daisy' (to 'Ode to the Gowdspink') and so forth. Burns repaid that debt handsomely when, in 1787, after his successful visit to the capital, he arranged for a stone to be erected over Fergusson's grave, which stands in Canongate Kirkyard to this day. His most touching comment on the dead poet was written the same year:

> O thou, my elder brother in misfortune,
> By far my elder brother in the Muse,
> With tears I pity thy unhappy fate!
> Why is the Bard unfitted for the world,
> Yet has so keen a relish of its pleasures?

Other writers, too, have found a kindred spirit in Fergusson's verses and in his tragic life. Stevenson gave instructions from Samoa for the gravestone to be repaired and re-inscribed, and toyed with the idea of dedicating the Edinburgh Edition of his own works to Fergusson's memory: "I had always a great sense of kinship with poor Robert Fergusson – so clever a boy, so wild, of such a mixed strain, so unfortunate, born in the same town with me, and, as I always felt, rather by express intimation than from evidence, so like myself."[37] He thought of himself, Fergusson and Burns as "three Robins who have touched the Scots lyre this last century". Burns, he wrote, was "for ever", but it was Fergusson he related to:

> Ah! what bonds we have – born in the same city; both sickly, both pestered, one nearly to madness, one to the madhouse, with a damnatory creed; both seeing the stars and the dawn, and wearing shoe-leather on the same ancient stones, under the same pends, down the same closes, where our common ancestors clashed in their armour, rusty or bright. And the old Robin, who was before Burns and the flood, died in his acute, painful youth, and left the models of the great things that were to come; and the new, who came after, outlived his green-sickness, and has faintly tried to parody the finished work... You will never know, nor will any man, how deep this feeling is: I believe Fergusson lives in me.[38]

In more recent times, a fourth Robin, Robert Garioch, also Edinburgh-born, acknowledged both the influence of and a deep affection for Fergusson, most notably in his poems 'At Robert Fergusson's Grave' and 'To Robert Fergusson'. In the latter, he wrote:

> Fergusson, tho twa-hunder year
> awa, your image is mair clear
> nor monie things that nou appear
>   in braid daylicht.
> What gars perspective turn sae queer?
>   What ails my sicht?
>
> Pairtlie, nae dout, because your een
> gey clearlie saw the Embro scene
> in times when Embro was a quean
>   sae weill worth seein
> that life wi her still had a wheen
>   guid things worth preein...
>
> And what a knack ye had of scrievin
> in caller verse yon rowth o levin,
> your wee stane warld, fechtin, thievin,
>   drinkin and swinkin,
> wi muckle fun and puckle grievin
>   and fowth of thinkin.

In these lines, Garioch takes us back to where we started: to the way in which Fergusson brought his own Auld Reikie alive. In 2004, Fergusson himself reappeared on the streets of his old city in the form of a bronze statue, by David Annand, depicting the poet striding down the Canongate. The statue, which was unveiled on 17th October that year, the anniversary of Fergusson's death, is located outside the Canongate kirkyard in which he is buried. It is a brilliant, life-affirming representation of Fergusson, and it reminds us that in the end, we should read Fergusson not because of how he died, but because of how he lived. Through his vibrant, reflective, streetwise, sophisticated, satirical and touching poetry, he lets us see, 250 years on, Edinburgh and Scotland as they then were, and as perhaps, in some ways, they still are.

The Robert Fergusson statue (by David Annand)
in the Canongate
Photo: Marianne Mitchelson

Notes
1. Alexander Grosart, *Robert Fergusson* (Edinburgh, 1898), p. 31.
2. Alexander Campbell, *An Introduction to the History of Scotch Poetry, from the 12th Century to this Time* (Edinburgh, 1798), p. 290.
3. Alexander Grosart, *op cit*, p. 46.
4. Alexander Grosart, *op cit*, p. 62.
5. Thomas Pennant, *A Tour in Scotland and Voyage to the Hebrides 1772* (Chester, 1774–76; Edinburgh, 1999 edition), p. 547.
6. Samuel Johnson, *A Journey to the Western Islands of Scotland* (London, 1775; Harmondsworth, 1984 edition with James Boswell, *Journal of a Tour to the Hebrides*), p. 39.
7. Alexander Grosart, *op cit*, p. 53.
8. *ibid*, p. 63.
9. Thomas Sommers, *The Life of Robert Fergusson, the Scottish Poet* (Edinburgh, 1803), p. 11.
10. These and other abusive comments appear in a copy of Fielding's *Miscellanies*, Vol. 3 (1732). The relevant pages are reproduced as Plates ii and iii in Robert Crawford (ed.), *Launch-Site for English Studies: Three Centuries of Literary Studies at the University of St Andrews* (St Andrews 1997). I am grateful to Professor Crawford for drawing my attention to them.
11. Alexander Campbell, *op cit*, p. 291.
12. Alexander Grosart, *op cit*, p. 82
13. Robert Chambers, *Traditions of Edinburgh* (Edinburgh, 1824, revised 1868; Edinburgh, 1980 edition), pp. 3–4.
14. Quoted in William Smellie, *Literary and Characteristic Lives of Gregory, Kames, Hume, and Smith* (Edinburgh, 1800), pp. 161–2.
15. Alexander Grosart, *op cit*, p. 89.
16. Robert Chambers, *op cit*, pp. 149–157.
17. Harry A. Cockburn, 'An Account of the Friday Club, Written by Lord Cockburn, Together with Notes on Certain Other Social Clubs in Edinburgh', in *The Book of the Old Edinburgh Club*, Vol. 3 (Edinburgh, 1910), pp. 155–6.
18. Matthew P. McDiarmid (ed.), *The Poems of Robert Fergusson* (Edinburgh, 1954–56), Vol. 1, p. 51.
19. Laing Collection, Edinburgh University Library, MS. II 334/2. The full text appears in McDiarmid's Scottish Text Society edition of Fergusson's *Poems*, Vol. 2, p. 168.

20. Thomas Sommers, *op cit*, p. 45.
21. *ibid*, pp. 27–8.
22. *The Works of Robert Fergusson, edited, with Life of the Author, and an Essay on his Genius and Writings by A.B.G.* [Alexander Grosart] (Edinburgh, 1851), pp. xci–xciii.
23. Matthew P. McDiarmid, *op cit*, Vol. 1, pp. 30–2.
24. Edwin Morgan, 'A Scottish Trawl', in Christopher Whyte (ed.), *Gendering the Nation* (Edinburgh, 1995), pp. 208–10.
25. James Inverarity, 'Strictures on Irving's Life of Fergusson', in *The Scots Magazine*, November 1801. Quoted in Matthew P. McDiarmid, *op cit*, Vol. 1, p. 67.
26. Alexander Campbell, *op cit*, p. 299.
27. Henry Mackenzie, *The Anecdotes and Egotisms of Henry Mackenzie 1745–1831* (H.W. Thompson (ed.), Oxford, 1927), p. 150.
28. Alexander Peterkin, *The Works of Robert Fergusson. To Which is Prefixed a Sketch of the Author's Life* (London, 1807), pp. 50, 54.
29. Thomas Sommers, *op cit*, pp. 29–30.
30. Quoted in Matthew P. McDiarmid, *op cit*, Vol. 1, p. 76.
31. *The Works of Robert Fergusson, edited, with Life of the Author, and an Essay on his Genius and Writings by A.B.G.* [Alexander Grosart] (Edinburgh, 1851), pp. xcvi–xcvii.
32. Thomas Sommers, *op cit*, pp. 33–6.
33. Billy Kay, *Scots: The Mither Tongue* (Edinburgh, 1986), pp. 90–1.
34. A study of this aspect of his work is to be found in F.W. Freeman, *Robert Fergusson and the Scots Humanist Compromise* (Edinburgh, 1984)
35. David Daiches, *Robert Fergusson* (Edinburgh, 1982), p. 86.
36. Matthew P. McDiarmid, *op cit*, Vol. 1, pp. 177–87.
37. Letter to Charles Baxter, May 1894.
38. Letter to W. Craibe Angus, April 1891.

Further Reading

Robert Crawford (ed.), *'Heaven-Taught Fergusson': Robert Burns's Favourite Scottish Poet* (East Linton, 2003)

David Daiches, *Robert Fergusson* (Edinburgh, 1982)

David Daiches, *The Paradox of Scottish Culture* (Oxford, 1964)

F.W. Freeman, *Robert Fergusson and the Scots Humanist Compromise* (Edinburgh, 1984)

Matthew P. McDiarmid (ed.), *The Poems of Robert Fergusson* (2 vols, Edinburgh, 1954–6)

Allan H. MacLaine, *Robert Fergusson* (New York, 1965)

Sydney Goodsir Smith (ed.), *Robert Fergusson 1750–1774: Essays by Various Hands to Commemorate the Bicentenary of his Birth* (Edinburgh, 1952)

Websites

The following two websites also contain useful information and further selections of Fergusson's work:

www.st-andrews.ac.uk/~www_se/fergusson/index.html
(dedicated website established by the St Andrews Scottish Studies Institute at the University of St Andrews)

www.robertfergusson.com
(website of the Robert Fergusson Society)

A Note on the Text

A major problem for any edition of Fergusson is that virtually none of his manuscripts survive. It is unclear what happened to them, although some were destroyed at the end of his life along with other papers: Grosart tells us that "the few unpublished MSS. which he had in his possession he committed to the flames" (*The Works of Robert Fergusson*, edited by Alexander Grosart, Edinburgh 1851, p. xcv). There is no evidence that the poet retrieved the manuscripts of poems printed in *The Weekly Magazine* from Walter Ruddiman's office. They were presumably lost or discarded there, or elsewhere at a later date.

The "original" texts for most of the poems therefore fall into two categories: the poems as first printed in *The Weekly Magazine*, *The Perth Magazine of Knowledge and Pleasure*, *The Dumfries Weekly Magazine* and elsewhere; and the poems as they appeared in the editions of 1773 and 1779. There is also the 1773 edition of *Auld Reikie*, minus its last forty lines. Over the years, many different selections of Fergusson have appeared, and almost all of them have departed from the texts as first published, sometimes substantially altering the orthography and vocabulary. This adulterating process was first corrected by Bruce Dickins in his 1925 reprint of the Scots poems, published by the Porpoise Press in Edinburgh, which relied on "the latest print which the author could possibly have overseen". Matthew P. McDiarmid's Scottish Text Society edition follows this principle.

There are, however, problems even with this approach. There is the preservation, for example, of what are almost certainly misprints or errors, either by Fergusson or the printers. As early as the 1779 edition, Matthew P. McDiarmid has noted, scant respect was paid by the Ruddimans to Fergusson's orthography and punctuation as found in *The Weekly Magazine*; but in the absence of manuscripts, we cannot be certain that the magazine did reproduce his writing with total accuracy. There is also the difficult question of how far Fergusson actually "oversaw" the printing process. He was only in his early twenties, he wrote some of his poems at great speed and must sometimes have delivered them for publication only a day, perhaps even only a few hours, before the magazine went to print. How rigorously would he have checked the presentation of his work, and how vociferously demanded corrections?

Then there is the matter of spelling. In the 1770s there was even less in the way of a Scots standard orthography than exists today, and Fergusson, while occasionally taking care (for example, over Aberdeenshire or Gaelic accents) with the spelling of certain pronunciations and dialect words, at other times is highly inconsistent. The word *bouk*, for example, meaning *body* or *person*, appears variously as *bouck*, *buick*, *buke* and *buik*. *Claes* for *clothes* also appears as *claise* and *clase*; and there is no obvious pattern in his choice of such spellings as *mak* or *make*, *bald*, *bauld* or *bawld*, or in his use of a *g* at the end of present participles. Sometimes an apostrophe is inserted where a Scots word has an English cognate that would seem to require one (*ha'e* for *have*, *awa'* for *away*), and sometimes it is not (*hae*, *awa*). This is utterly typical of the period, when spelling even in English was very individualistic: add in Scots, which was frequently represented by what we now regard as English spellings (*night* for *nicht*, *town* for *toun*) and the scope for confusion is easily apparent. As Albert D. Mackie has written, in the essay mentioned at the end of this note, Fergusson "relied on his Scottish readers knowing how the words were expected to be pronounced, but a reader not of his day might be excused for getting hopelessly bogged down among these 'ous' and 'ows'."

I have therefore departed from the principle kept to by Dickins and McDiarmid, for three reasons. First, this is not, and is not intended to be, an academic or definitive text. That, in my opinion, already exists in McDiarmid, for those who require it. Second, the "original" text, as indicated above, is hardly ever demonstrably Fergusson's version anyway. Third, the passage of time has meant that modern readers are very often tripped up or fooled by the text into mispronunciation or even misreading. Here are two examples: in the first poem, the 'Elegy, on the Death of Mr David Gregory', the first six stanzas end with the word *dead*, which it is clear from the rhyme pattern should be pronounced *deid*. This is now the accepted Scots spelling and I see no reason why modern readers should be distracted by seeing *dead* from reading and pronouncing the word as Fergusson intended it. The second example involves words like *grien* for *yearn*, which in the original text is spelt *green* in the phrase "If ony mettl'd stirrah green" in 'Braid Claith', and *siclike* for *thus*, which is spelt *sicklike* in 'To My Auld Breeks'. In both instances (and in others) leaving such spellings unaltered is extremely misleading, and I have changed them accordingly.

I have removed most of the italics and capitalisation used for emphasis, except where their retention seems essential. I have also dropped all "apologetic apostrophes" (from forms such as *ha'e* and *wi'*), retaining them only for clarity in forms like *o'*, *a'* and *an'*, and I have opted for some spellings, like *owr*, *ee* and *loun*, as against *o'er*, *eie* and *lown*. In almost all cases the spellings chosen were used at least once by Fergusson. I have not, however, eradicated all his inconsistencies, especially where there is any doubt about pronunciation: to do so would be to diminish the flavour of the poems and of the period, would occasionally eliminate deliberate subtleties, and in some cases would introduce further complications. It must be remembered that Fergusson did not write in a single local dialect, but that his Scots contains both spoken and literary elements, and draws on words and pronunciations from Edinburgh, the Lothians, Fife, the North-East and elsewhere. There are too many emendations to list, and so they remain "silent", but I have certainly not tried to make his poems adhere to some suppositional *Scots* standard. Basically, my principle has been to upgrade the text sensitively, in order to present as readable and accessible a version of Fergusson's poems for the modern reader as possible. I repeat, this is a text intended primarily not for academics, but for general readers. It is they who have missed out on reading Fergusson in recent years, and I hope this edition takes a step in returning him to them.

As a rough guide, Scots speakers will find that, as with Burns, applying Scots pronunciations to Fergusson's words, even when they appear to be printed as English ones, will usually bring out the best of his rhymes and rhythms. An excellent essay covering many of the issues discussed here is Albert D. Mackie's 'Fergusson's Language: Braid Scots Then and Now' in Sydney Goodsir Smith (ed.), *Robert Fergusson 1750–1774: Essays by Various Hands to Commemorate the Bicentenary of his Birth* (Edinburgh, 1952).

Notes on the Illustrations

All the illustrations come from the work of John Kay (1742–1826), who kept a barber's shop in Edinburgh's Parliament Square until 1785, when he decided to concentrate full-time on his caricatures of city characters. He drew some 900 portraits, 361 of which appeared in two volumes in 1837–38, published by Hugh Paton under the title *A Series of Original Portraits and Caricature Etchings, by the late John Kay, miniature painter, Edinburgh; with biographical sketches and illustrative anecdotes*. The extensive notes were researched and written by one James Paterson, whom Paton paid 15s per week for his work, and were then edited by an advocate named James Maidment. Although from a slightly later period than Fergusson, Kay's etchings, and their accompanying text, are an invaluable source of information about Edinburgh in the whole 18th century. The following notes, relating to the illustrations reproduced in this book, are taken from *Original Portraits*, but are only a fraction of the wonderful material to be found there.

John Dhu, or Shon Dow, a stalwart of the City Guard, 1784
(page 55)

"John, a Highlander by birth, was conspicuous for his peculiarly robust and rough appearance, which was of itself as effectual in keeping the younger and more mischievous part of the population in awe, as any ten Lochaber axes in the corps. The author of *Waverley* speaks of him somewhere, as one of the fiercest-looking fellows he had ever seen. In facing the unruly mob of those days, John had shown such a degree of valour as to impress the Magistrates with a high sense of his utility as a public servant... On one occasion, about the time of the French Revolution, when the Town-Guard had been signalising the King's birth-day by firing in the Parliament Square, being unusually pressed and insulted by the populace, this undaunted warrior turned upon one peculiarly outrageous member of the democracy, and, with one blow of his battle-axe, laid him lifeless on the causey...

"Although he had been an undaunted soldier, and was a terror to the mobocracy of Edinburgh, he was altogether a man of kind feelings, and by no means overstepped the limits of his duty, unless very much provoked. Many yet remember his conduct towards those young delinquents, whose petty depredations brought them under his surveillance. After detaining them in the guard-house for a short time, and having administered a little wholesome terror, by way of caution, should they 'ever do the like again', *Shon* would open the half-door of the guard-room, and push them out with a gentle slap on the breech, saying – 'There noo, pe off; an' I'll say you'll didna rin awa',' – meaning that he would make an excuse for them."

Colonel Munro, a well-known blue-gown beggar, 1801
(page 62)

"The name of 'Colonel Munro', as applied to a half-crazed old man who used to frequent the streets of Edinburgh, is familiar to many of the older inhabitants, but almost nothing is known of his history. He obtained the *soubriquet* of 'Colonel' from having fought under the banners of Prince Charles Edward; and to the last he continued to profess his devotion to the house of Stuart. In token of his sympathy for the fallen race, he always wore a white cockade in his bonnet or hat. His Jacobitical predilections, however, did not prevent him from participating in the bounty of the reigning dynasty; hence the lines of the artist –

'Behold, couragious Collonel Monro,
A Highland hero, turn'd a Blue Goun beau.'"

A fisher-wife selling oysters, in traditional striped dress, 1812
(page 66)

"The artist has not favoured us with the name of the 'Oyster Lass' whom this figure represents. The omission is probably a matter of no great moment, as the characteristics of individuals of her class are usually pretty much the same... Stout, clean, and blooming, if they are not the most handsome or comely of Eve's daughters, they are at least the most perfect pictures of robust and vigorous health; and not a few of them, under the pea-jacket and superabundance of petticoat with which they load themselves, conceal a symmetry of form that might excite the envy of a Duchess."

A fashionable company promenading on North Bridge, 1784
(page 79)

"William Doyle, Samuel Sone, and William Foster. The first of these figures to the left was a Lieutenant Doyle; the centre one, Mr Sone, a surgeon, commonly called 'The Little Doctor'; and the third, Captain Foster, all of the 24th Regiment; the two last were inseparable companions, notwithstanding their disparity in point of size.

"While here with the regiment in 1784, they were remarkable for their attention to the fair sex; Mr Kay has accordingly represented them as squiring three of the most celebrated belles of the day, dressed in the fashion of the time, along the North Bridge."

Three Captains of the City Guard, 1786
(page 93)

"George Pitcairn, George Robertson, Robert Pillans. These three persons were all, as announced in the title, Captains of the Old Edinburgh City Guard. This appointment was not generally held by military men, and it was frequently conferred upon decaying burgesses, whose character recommended them to the patronage of the Magistrates, and whose circumstances rendered this tolerably lucrative situation (which was *ad vitam aut culpam*) an object of some moment...

"Captain Pitcairn had originally been a cloth-merchant in the city, and had more than once served in the Magistracy. Having subsequently become embarrassed in his circumstances, he was appointed, on a vacancy occurring, to the Captaincy of the City Guard; but, engaging some time afterwards in no very creditable speculation, he lost both his situation and his character...

"Robertson, the second figure in the Print, had been an officer in the Dutch service previous to his appointment to a command in the City Guard, and was selected for the latter office with the view of improving the discipline and general military character of the corps. Of his private history nothing is known, nor was his professional career as a civic soldier, which was very brief, distinguished by any remarkable event...

"Pillans, the third figure, was originally a brewer in the vicinity of the city, and was for some time one of the resident bailies of the then suburban districts of Potterrow and Portsburgh. It is alleged, that the gallant Captain was fully as dexterous at handling a bottle as a sword; and a certain rotundity observable in the accompanying likeness of him would indeed, seem to favour the insinuation...

"This Print is entitled 'Three Captains of Pilate's Guard', in allusion to a popular fiction, that the City of Edinburgh had a town-guard before the birth of our Saviour; and that three of that body had joined the Roman troops after the invasion of Britain by Julius Caesar, and were actually present with Pilate's troops at the Crucifixion."

The City Guardhouse, which stood in the High Street till 1785 (etching made in 1786), *(page 121)*

"This dingy, mean-looking edifice... was a slated building, one storey in height, and consisted of four apartments. On the west and south-west corner was the Captain's Room; and, adjoining, on the north, was a place for prisoners, called the 'Burgher's Room'. In the centre was the common hall; and, on the east, the apartment devoted to the city chimney-sweepers, who were called 'tron men' – two figures of whom will be observed in the engraving. The extreme length of the structure, from east to west, was seventy feet, and the breadth forty over the walls. The floor, with the exception of the Captain's Room, was composed of flags, under which was a vaulted cell, called the 'Black Hole', where coals for the use of the Guard-House were kept, and into which refractory prisoners were put.

"The wooden mare at the west end of the building was placed there for the purpose of punishing such soldiers as might be found guilty of misdemeanours. The delinquent, with a gun tied to each foot, was mounted for a certain period, proportioned to the extent of his offence, and exposed to the gaze and derision of the populace, who sometimes were not idle spectators of the exhibition. The figure bestriding the 'wooden mare' is merely intended to represent the nature of the punishment.

"Over the half-door of the Guard-House will be distinguished the well-known John Dhu. John, who was a corporal of the Guard, is here in the position which he daily occupied, ready to receive, with a 'Highland curse', whoever was unfortunate enough to be committed to his surveillance. The rank of the offender made no difference – rich and poor met with the same reception. A chronicle of the beaux and belles, who found a night's shelter within its walls, would no doubt be gratifying to the lovers of antiquated scandal.

"The Guard-House, situated in the very centre of the main street, was unquestionably both an eye-sore and an inconvenience... In 1785, it was resolved that the obnoxious building should cease to exist."

Captain James Burnet, last Captain of the City Guard, 1814 (page 157)

"Captain Burnet was a native of East Lothian. He was one of the Captains of the Guard who had not previously been in the army; and, if we except his experience as a member of the First Regiment of Edinburgh Volunteers, may be supposed to have been a novice in military matters. Previous to his appointment, he kept a grocer's shop at the head of the Fleshmarket Close.

"The personal appearance of Mr Burnet is well delineated in the Portrait. He was a man of great bulk; and when in his best days, weighed upwards of nineteen stone...

"Few men of his time enjoyed their bottle with greater zest than Captain Burnet; and at the civic feasts, with which these palmy times abounded, no one did greater execution with the knife and fork. He seldom retired with less than two bottles under his belt, and that too without at all deranging the order of his 'upper storey'. 'Two-and-a-half here,' was a frequent exclamation, as he clapped his hand on his portly paunch, if he chanced to meet a quondam *bon vivant*, on his way home from the festive board."

Elegy, on the Death of Mr David Gregory, Late Professor of Mathematics in the University of St Andrews

Now mourn, ye college masters a'!
And frae your een a tear lat fa,
Fam'd Gregory death has taen awa
    Without remeid;[1]
The skaith ye've met wi's nae that sma,
    Sin Gregory's deid.

The students too will miss him sair,
To school them weel his eident care,
Now they may mourn for ever mair,
    They hae great need;

There is little doubt that this, Fergusson's earliest surviving work, was written in 1765 when he was fourteen and in his first year as a student at St Andrews. It appeared in the first, 1773 edition of his poems, *Poems by Robert Fergusson*, printed by Walter & Thomas Ruddiman, Edinburgh.

David Gregory was a member of the extensive Gregory dynasty, originally from Aberdeenshire, which produced several distinguished physicians and mathematicians over a period of more than two centuries. He succeeded his father Charles in the Chair of Mathematics in 1739, resigning at the end of the 1763–4 session. Fergusson, who began at St Andrews in November 1764, would not therefore have attended his lectures. Gregory died on 13 April 1765, and this presumably occasioned the composition of the poem.

1 **without remeid**: without remedy, or, more specifically in a legal sense, without redress of one's grievances through appeal to a higher authority. Fergusson is consciously echoing a phrase used in the mock-elegiac poems which were his models: it appears in the first stanzas of Robert Sempill of Beltrees's 'Epitaph on Sanny Briggs' and William Hamilton of Gilbertfield's 'The Last Dying Words of Bonny Heck, a Famous Greyhound in the Shire of Fife', and in stanza 13 of Allan Ramsay's 'Elegy on Maggy Johnston'.

They'll hip the maist feck o' their lear,[2]
    Sin Gregory's deid.

He could, by Euclid, prove[3] lang syne
A ganging point compos'd a line;
By numbers too he could divine,
    Whan he did read,
That three times three just made up nine;
    But now he's deid.

In Algebra weel skill'd he was,
An' kent fu weel proportion's laws;
He could make clear baith B's and A's[4]
    Wi his lang heid;[5]
Rin owr surd roots,[6] but[7] cracks or flaws;
    But now he's deid.

Weel vers'd was he in architecture,
An' kent the nature o' the sector,

---

2 **They'll hip the maist feck o' their lear**: they'll miss the biggest part of their education.
3 **He could, by Euclid, prove**: Euclid (fl. 300 BC) was the founder of classical geometry. His *Elements* were a standard work on the subject until the 20th century. According to Newtonian mathematical theory, magnitudes are generated by motion. "A ganging point compos'd a line" succinctly encapsulates this concept. While Newton's ideas were initially opposed by many academics in England, they had been quickly and warmly received in Scotland, in part thanks to the influence of the earlier Gregories.
4 **He could make clear baith B's and A's**: the rhyme sequence makes clear that "A's" is pronounced *aws* in the old Scots manner. Some fifty years later, it was still common. Confusion between Hugh Miller's own similarly broad pronunciation of the alphabet and his master's more modern rendition would precipitate the fight between them which marked the end of Miller's formal schooling. See Miller, *My Schools and Schoolmasters* (1854), ch.7.
5 **Wi his lang heid**: with his great intelligence. "Lang-heidit", still current, means "shrewd, sagacious".
6 **surd roots**: roots that cannot be expressed in rational numbers.
7 **but**: without.

Upon baith globes[8] he weel could lecture,
      An' gar's tak heed;
Of geometry he was the Hector;
      But now he's deid.

Sae weel's he'd fley the students a',
Whan they war skelpin at the ba,
They took leg bail[9] and ran awa,
      Wi pith and speed;
We winna get a sport sae braw
      Sin Gregory's deid.

Great 'casion hae we a' to weep,
An' cleed our skins in mourning deep,
For Gregory death will fairly keep
      To take his nap;
He'll till the resurrection sleep
      As sound's a tap.

---

8 **baith globes**: i.e. the terrestrial and celestial globes.
9 **leg bail**: flight from justice.

The Daft-Days

Now mirk December's dowie face
Glowrs owr the rigs wi sour grimace,
While, thro' his *minimum* of space,
    The bleer-ey'd sun,
Wi blinkin light and stealing pace,
    His race doth run.

From naked groves nae birdie sings,
To shepherd's pipe nae hillock rings,
The breeze nae od'rous flavour brings
    From Borean[1] cave,
And dwyning nature droops her wings,
    Wi visage grave.

Mankind but scanty pleasure glean
Frae snawy hill or barren plain,
Whan winter, 'midst his nipping train,
    Wi frozen spear,
Sends drift owr a' his bleak domain,
    And guides the weir.

Auld Reikie![2] thou'rt the canty hole,
A bield for mony caldrife soul,
Wha snugly at thine ingle loll,

First published in *The Weekly Magazine*, 2 January 1772. The Daft Days are the New Year holidays.

1 **Borean**: of the north. In Greek mythology, Boreas was the god of the north wind, and the wind itself.
2 **Auld Reikie**: Edinburgh, so-called because the city's smoke was visible for miles, especially from across the Forth in Fife. The oldest published use of the nickname recorded by the *Scottish National Dictionary* is in Ramsay's 'Elegy on Maggy Johnston' (1712).

      Baith warm and couth,
While round they gar the bicker roll
      To weet their mouth.

When merry Yule-day comes, I trou,
You'll scantlins find a hungry mou;
Sma are our cares, our stamacks fou
      O' gusty gear,
And kickshaws, strangers to our view,
      Sin fairn-year.

Ye browster wives, now busk ye braw,
And fling your sorrows far awa;
Then come and gie's the tither blaw
      Of reaming ale,
Mair precious than the well of Spa,[3]
      Our hearts to heal.

Then, tho' at odds wi a' the warl',
Amang oursels we'll never quarrel;
Tho' Discord gie a canker'd snarl
      To spoil our glee,
As lang's there's pith into the barrel
      We'll drink and 'gree.

Fidlers, your pins in temper fix,
And roset weel your fiddle-sticks;
But banish vile Italian tricks
      Frae out your *quorum*,
Nor *fortes* wi *pianos* mix –
      Gie's *Tulloch Gorum*.[4]

---

3 **Spa**: the Belgian watering-place from which the word derives.
4 **Tulloch Gorum**: the gloss given in the 1773 *Poems* is "Name of a tune". It would seem that Fergusson's reference to it inspired the Rev. John Skinner to put words to the tune. Skinner's words appeared in *The Weekly Magazine* of 2 May 1776, prefaced by this stanza from Fergusson. The same patriotic defence of Scots song and music against ubiquitous "dringing dull Italian lays" is evident.

For nought can cheer the heart sae weel
As can a canty Highland reel;
It even vivifies the heel
    To skip and dance:
Lifeless is he wha canna feel
    Its influence.

Let mirth abound, let social cheer
Invest the dawning of the year;
Let blithesome innocence appear
    To crown our joy;
Nor envy wi sarcastic sneer
    Our bliss destroy.

And thou, great god of *Aqua Vitae*!
Wha sways the empire of this city,
When fou we're sometimes capernoity,
    Be thou prepar'd
To hedge us frae that black banditti,
    The City Guard.[5]

    Burns described Skinner's creation as "the best Scotch song Scotland ever saw".

[5] **City Guard**: "Guard" should of course be pronounced *Guaird*. This notorious law enforcement body was composed mainly of retired soldiers of the Highland regiments. According to Walter Scott, being Highlanders they were "neither by birth, education, or former habits, trained to endure with much patience the insults of the rabble, or the provoking petulance of truant schoolboys, and idle debauchees of all descriptions, with whom their occupation brought them into contact". The Gaelic poet Duncan Bàn Macintyre served in the Guard from 1766 to 1793. A city police force was established in 1805. Fergusson, Scott says, mentions the City Guard so often in his poems that "he may be termed their poet laureate". See Scott, *The Heart of Midlothian* (1818), ch.3.

*John Dhu, or Shon Dow,
a stalwart of the City Guard, 1784*

Elegy, on the Death of Scots Music

> Mark it, Caesario; it is old and plain.
> The spinsters and the knitters in the sun,
> And the free maids that weave their thread with bones,
> Do use to chant it.
> —*Shakespeare's Twelfth Night*

On Scotia's plains, in days of yore,
When lads and lasses tartan[1] wore,
Saft Music rang on ilka shore,
    In hamely weed;
But harmony is now no more,
    And music deid.

Round her the feather'd choir would wing,
Sae bonnily she wont to sing,
And sleely wake the sleeping string,
    Their sang to lead,
Sweet as the zephyrs of the spring;
    But now she's deid.

Mourn ilka nymph and ilka swain,
Ilk sunny hill and dowie glen;
Let weeping streams and Naiads drain
    Their fountain heid;
Let echo swell the dolefu strain,
    Since music's deid.

First published in *The Weekly Magazine*, 5 March 1772. The quotation from *Twelfth Night* is from Act II, scene iv.

1 **tartan**: Allan Ramsay's 'Tartana' (1718) had praised the humble plaid in English heroic couplets. At the time of Fergusson's poem, the statute proscribing Highland dress in the aftermath of the 'Forty-five was still in force, and would not be repealed till 1782.

Whan the saft vernal breezes ca[2]
The grey-hair'd winter's fogs awa,
Naebody than is heard to blaw
    Near hill or mead,
On chaunter, or on aiten straw,
    Since music's deid.

Nae lasses now, on simmer days,
Will lilt at bleaching of their claes;
Nae herds on Yarrow's bonny braes,
    Or banks of Tweed,[3]
Delight to chant their hameil lays,
    Since music's deid.

At gloamin now the bagpipe's dumb,
Whan weary owsen hameward come;
Sae sweetly as it wont to bum,
    And *pibrachs* skreed;
We never hear its warlike hum;
    For music's deid.

Macgibbon's gane:[4] Ah! wae's my heart!
The man in music maist expert,
Wha could sweet melody impart,
    And tune the reed,
Wi sic a slee and pawky art;
    But now he's deid.

---

2 **ca**: drive.
3 **on Yarrow's bonny braes, or banks of Tweed**: the allusions are to William Hamilton of Bangour's ballad 'The Braes of Yarrow' and to either James Hook's 'The Banks of Tweed' or Robert Crawfurd's 'Tweed-Side'.
4 **Macgibbon's gane**: William Macgibbon (c.1695–1756) was the leading Scottish composer of his age, and principal violinist to the Edinburgh Musical Society. He published three collections of *Scots Tunes* for fiddle between 1742 and 1755, and this is the reason for Fergusson's praise. Ironically, Macgibbon, although applauded by patriots as a folk-composer, was also a master of continental styles, and of the Italianate ornamentation which Fergusson attacks.

Ilk carline now may grunt and grane,
Ilk bonny lassie make great mane,
Since he's awa, I trou there's nane
    Can fill his steid;
The blythest sangster on the plain!
    Alake, he's deid!

Now foreign sonnets bear the gree,
And crabbit queer variety
Of sound fresh sprung frae Italy,
    A bastard breed!
Unlike that saft-tongu'd melody
    Which now lies deid.

Could lav'rocks at the dawning day,
Could linties chirming frae the spray,
Or todling burns that smoothly play
    Owr gowden bed,
Compare wi *Birks of Invermay?*[5]
    But now they're dead.

O Scotland! that could yence afford
To bang[6] the pith of Roman sword,
Winna your sons, wi joint accord,
    To battle speed?
And fight till music be restor'd,
    Which now lies deid.

---

[5] **Birks of Invermay**: the tune was published in 1733 in William Thomson's *Orpheus Caledonius*, Vol.2 (1733), a work which put tunes to the ballads and songs printed by Allan Ramsay in his *Tea-Table Miscellany*. David Mallet or Malloch had already written English words for the tune, which appeared in the *Miscellany*'s third volume (1727). Fergusson's friend and biographer Thomas Sommers called him "the best singer of the *Birks of Invermay* I ever heard".

[6] **bang**: beat, overcome.

The King's Birth-Day in Edinburgh

> Oh! qualis hurly-burly fuit, si forte vidisses.
> —*Polemo-Middinia*

I sing the day sae aften sung,
Wi which our lugs hae yearly rung,
In whase loud praise the Muse has dung
    A' kind o' print;
But wow! the limmer's fairly flung;
    There's naething in't.

First published in *The Weekly Magazine*, 4 June 1772. King George III celebrated his 34th birthday on this day. Fergusson's poem must therefore have been based on the experiences of previous years, which, judging from the report in *The Weekly Magazine* of 10 June 1773 on *that* year's events, were of a pattern. This report notes the firing of guns from the Castle, approvingly describes the Lord Provost's procession and loyal toasts drunk by the great and good, and adds that "the evening concluded with a brilliant assembly. It is, however, to be regretted, that, on such days of festivity, the lower class of people seldom indulge their mirth without mischief. On this occasion they became, towards the evening, perfectly licentious, and, after their ammunition of squibs and crackers was exhausted, they employed dead cats, mud &c. which they discharged very plentifully on the city guard; and, when threatened to be chastised or apprehended, they betook themselves to the more dangerous weapons of stones and brickbats, &c. In this encounter several of the guard were wounded, and they in return dealt their blows pretty liberally, by which, amid the confusion, some innocent persons suffered along with the guilty."

The epigraph is from William Drummond of Hawthornden's comic poem 'Polemo-Middinia' ('The Midden Fecht'), a macaronic tour-de-force composed about 1645 in a dense mixture of Scoto-Latin, or Latino-Scots. It was very popular in Fergusson's day and several editions existed. The epigraph conflates two lines (112 and 115) of the poem, and translates as "Oh, what a hurly-burly there was, if you had but seen it". A modern edition (with English translation) of Drummond's poem can be found in Allan H. MacLaine (ed.), *The Christis Kirk Tradition: Scots Poems of Folk Festivity* (Glasgow, 1996).

I'm fain to think the joy's the same
In London town as here at hame,
Whare fock of ilka age and name,
    Baith blind and cripple,
Forgather aft, O fy for shame!
    To drink and tipple.

O Muse, be kind, and dinna fash us
To flee awa beyont Parnassus,[1]
Nor seek for Helicon[2] to wash us,
    That heath'nish spring;
Wi Highland whisky scour our hawses,
    And gar us sing.

Begin then, dame, ye've drunk your fill,
You wouldna hae the tither gill?
You'll trust me, mair would do you ill,
    And ding you doitet:
Troth 'twould be sair agains my will
    To hae the wyte o't.

Sing then, how, on the fourth of June,
Our bells screed aff a loyal tune,
Our ancient castle shoots at noon,
    Wi flag-staff buskit,
Frae which the soldier blades come doun
    To cock their musket.

Oh willawins! Mons Meg,[3] for you,

---

[1] **Parnassus:** a mountain near Delphi, consecrated to Apollo and the Muses and hence the seat of poetry and music.
[2] **Helicon:** the home of the Muses, containing the fountains of Aganippe and Hippocrene, hence the source of poetic inspiration.
[3] **Mons Meg:** the huge siege-gun, probably made at Mons in Flanders, which was given to James II in 1457 by Philip of Burgundy. It was used by James IV at the siege of Norham Castle in 1497. It weighs five tons and could fire heavy shot a distance of two miles. It burst when it was overcharged to fire a salute to the Duke of York in 1681. Removed to the Tower of London after the 'Forty-five, it

'Twas firing crack'd thy muckle mou;
What black mishanter gart ye spew
    Baith gut and gaw?
I fear they bang'd thy belly fu
    Against the law.

Right seldom am I gien to bannin,
But, by my saul, ye was a cannon,
Could hit a man had he been stannin
    In shire o' Fife,
Sax lang Scots miles ayont Clackmannan,
    And tak his life.

The hills in terror would cry out,
And echo to thy dinsome rout;
The herds would gather in their nowt,
    That glowr'd wi wonder,
Haflins afraid to bide thereout
    To hear thy thunder.

Sing likewise, Muse, how blue-gown bodies,[4]
Like scar-craws new taen down frae woodies,
Come here to cast their clouted duddies,
    And get their pay:
Than them, what magistrate mair proud is
    On king's birth-day?

On this great day the city-guard,
In military art well-lear'd,

---

    stayed there until a successful campaign by Sir Walter Scott for the return of "the old murderess" saw it restored to Edinburgh Castle in 1829, where it has remained to this day. Fergusson's verses, then, lament a famous object he had never seen.

[4] **blue-gown bodies**: professional beggars, distinguished by their long blue gowns. Edie Ochiltree, in Scott's *The Antiquary* (1816), is described as "one of that privileged class which are called in Scotland the King's Bedes-men, or, vulgarly, Blue-gowns" (ch.4).

*Colonel Munro, a well-known
blue-gown beggar, 1801*

Wi powder'd pow and shaven beard,
    Gang thro' their functions,
By hostile rabble seldom spar'd
    Of clarty unctions.

O soldiers! for your ain dear sakes,
For Scotland's, alias Land of Cakes,[5]
Gie not her bairns sic deadly pakes,
    Nor be sae rude,
Wi firelock or Lochaber aix,[6]
    As spill their blude.

Now round and round the serpents[7] whiz,
Wi hissing wrath and angry phiz;
Sometimes they catch a gentle gizz,
    Alake the day!
And singe, wi hair-devouring bizz,
    Its curls away.

Should th' owner patiently keek round,
To view the nature of his wound,
Dead pussie, dragled thro' the pond,
    Takes him a lounder,
Which lays his honour on the ground
    As flat's a flounder.

---

5 **Land of Cakes**: Scotland. A phrase also used by Burns, first recorded in the mid-17th century. It refers to oatmeal cakes.
6 **Lochaber aix**: a long-handled battle-axe, with a hook at the back of the hatchet, with which the user could grapple the top of a gate or wall and pull himself over.
7 **serpents**: fireworks, of a type which zig-zagged like a snake, and was a menace to wigs and other headgear. In his *Journal* for 9 March 1829, Walter Scott records that at the parade celebrating the return of Mons Meg "my daughter had what might have proved a frightful accident. Some rockets were let off, one of which lighted upon her head, and set her bonnet on fire. She neither screamed nor ran, but quietly permitted Charles Sharpe to extinguish the fire, which he did with great coolness and dexterity."

The Muse maun also now implore
Auld wives to steek ilk hole and bore;
If baudrins[8] slip but to the door,
  I fear, I fear,
She'll no lang shank upon all-four
   This time o' year.

Next day each hero tells his news
O' crackit crowns and broken broos,
And deeds that here forbid the Muse
  Her theme to swell,
Or time mair precious abuse
   Their crimes to tell.

She'll rather to the fields resort,
Whare music gars the day seem short,
Whare doggies play, and lambies sport,
  On gowany braes,
Whare peerless Fancy hads her court,
   And tunes her lays.

---

[8] **baudrins**: pet name for a cat. The practice of flinging dead cats during public commotions seems to have been common. For an excellent example, see John Galt's novel *The Provost* (1822), ch.10.

CALLER OYSTERS

> Happy the man who, free from care and strife,
> In silken or in leathern purse retains
> A splendid shilling. He nor hears with pain
> New oysters cry'd, nor sighs for chearful ale.
> —*Philips*

Of a' the waters that can hobble
A fishin yole or salmon coble,
And can reward the fisher's trouble,
    Or south or north,[1]
There's nane sae spacious and sae noble
    As Firth o' Forth.

In her the skate and codlin sail,
The eel fou souple wags her tail,
Wi herrin, fleuk and mackarel,
    And whitens dainty:
Their spindle-shanks the labsters trail,
    Wi partans plenty.

Auld Reikie's sons blyth faces wear;
September's merry month is near,
That brings in Neptune's[2] caller cheer,
    New oysters fresh;
The halesomest and nicest gear
    Of fish or flesh.

First published in *The Weekly Magazine*, 27 August 1772. The motto is from the opening lines of 'The Splendid Shilling', a Miltonic burlesque by the Oxfordshire-born poet John Philips (1676–1709).

The Forth held some of the greatest concentrations of oysters in Europe, and the beds seemed inexhaustible. In Fergusson's day, up to thirty million oysters a year were taken for consumption in London, Holland, and of course locally. Over-fishing and pollution wiped out the oysters in the Forth in the 19th century.

1 **Or south or north**: either south or north.
2 **Neptune**: the Roman god of the sea.

*A fisher-wife selling oysters,
in traditional striped dress, 1812*

O! then we needna gie a plack
For dand'ring mountebank or quack,
Wha o' their drogs sae bauldly crack,
    And spred sic notions,
As gar their feckless patient tak
    Their stinkin potions.

Come prie, frail man! for gin thou art sick,
The oyster is a rare cathartic,
As ever doctor patient gart lick
    To cure his ails;
Whether you hae the head or heart-ake,
    It ay prevails.

Ye tiplers, open a' your poses,
Ye wha are faush'd wi plouky noses!
Fling owr your craig sufficient doses,
    You'll thole a hunder,
To fleg awa your simmer roses,[3]
    And naething under.

Whan big as burns the gutters rin,
Gin ye hae catcht a droukit skin,
To Luckie Middlemist's[4] loup in,

---

3 **simmer roses**: a rash or skin eruption caused by too much drink.
4 **Luckie Middlemist's**: a popular tavern in the Cowgate. Luckie Middlemist or Middlemass was the landlady (Luckie being the familiar term for an elderly woman or innkeeper). Of such establishments, Hugo Arnot in his *History of Edinburgh* (1788) writes, "there is a species of taverns of a lower denomination, which, however, are sometimes resorted to by good company, when disposed to enjoy a frolic. These are the oyster-cellars, a sort of ale-houses, where the proper entertainment of the house is oysters, punch and porter... Most of the oyster-cellars have a sort of long-room, where a small party may enjoy the exercise of a country dance, to the music of a fiddle, harp, or bag-pipe. But the equivocal character of these houses of resort prevents them from being visited by any of the fair sex who seek the praise of delicacy, or pique themselves on propriety of conduct." (p.354)

        And sit fu snug
Owr oysters and a dram o' gin,
          Or haddock lug.

When auld Saunt Giles, at aucht o'clock,
Gars merchant louns their chopies lock,
There we adjourn wi hearty fock
          To birl our bodles,
And get wharewi to crack our joke,
          And clear our noddles.

Whan Phoebus[5] did his windocks steek,
How aften at that ingle cheek
Did I my frosty fingers beek,
          And taste gude fare!
I trou there was nae hame to seek
          Whan steghin there.

While glakit fools, owr rife o' cash,
Pamper their weyms wi fousom trash,
I think a chiel may gayly pass;
          He's no ill boden
That gusts his gab wi oyster sauce,
          And hen weel soden.

At Musselbrough, and eke Newhaven,
The fisher-wives will get top livin,
When lads gang out on Sunday's even
          To treat their joes,
And tak of fat pandours[6] a prieven,
          Or mussel brose.

---

5 **Phoebus**: an epithet (Greek, The Shining One) for Apollo, god of the sun. Hence, the sun itself.
6 **pandours**: large, especially succulent oysters, found around Preston*pans*.

Than sometimes ere they flit their doup,
They'll ablins a' their siller coup
For liquor clear frae cutty stoup,
    To weet their wizen,
And swallow owr a dainty soup,
    For fear they gizzen.

A' ye wha canna stand sae sicker,
Whan twice you've toom'd the big-ars'd bicker,
Mix caller oysters wi your liquor,
    And I'm your debtor,
If greedy priest or drouthy vicar
    Will thole it better.

Epistles Between J.S. and Robert Fergusson

TO MR ROBERT FERGUSSON

Is Allan risen frae the deid,
Wha aft has tun'd the aiten reed,[1]
And by the muses was decreed
    To grace the thistle?
Na; Fergusson's cum in his steid
    To blaw the whistle.

In troth, my callant, I'm sae fain
To see your sonsy, canty strain,
You write sic easy stile and plain,
    And words sae bonny,
Nae suth'ron loun dare you disdain,
    Or cry *fy on ye*.

Whae'er has at *Auld Reikie* been,
And king's birth-days exploits has seen,
Maun own that ye hae gien a keen
    And true description;
Nor say ye've at Parnassus been
    To form a fiction.

  First published in *The Weekly Magazine*, 3 September 1772. The author of this address was, according to A. B. Grosart's biography (1898) of Fergusson in the *Famous Scots* series published by Oliphant, Anderson & Ferrier, "probably John Scott, a farmer", but no more information is given. Although the poem is signed from Berwick, the writer calls himself "Mid-Louthian Johnnie", which implies that he had at some point moved from near Edinburgh to the Borders.

1 **the aiten reed:** references to shepherds' pipes, whistles and suchlike entirely accord with the conventions of pastoral verse. It was in this "school", typified by Allan (referred to in the first line) Ramsay's hugely popular rustic comedy *The Gentle Shepherd* (1725), that Fergusson's admirers placed him.

Hale be your heart, ye canty chield!
May ye ne'er want a gude warm bield,
And sic gude cakes as Scotland yields,
      And ilka dainty
That grows or feeds upon her fields,
      And whisky plenty.

But ye, perhaps, thirst mair for fame
Than a' the gude things I can name,
And then ye will be sair to blame
      My gude intention:
For that ye needna gae frae hame,
      Ye've sic pretension.

Sae saft and sweet your verses jingle,
And your auld words sae meetly mingle,
'Twill gar baith married fouk and single
      To roose your lays;
When we forgether round the ingle,
      We'll chant your praise.

When I again Auld Reikie see,
And can forgether, lad, with thee,
Then we wi muckle mirth and glee
      Shall tak a gill,
And of your *caller oysters* we
      Shall eat our fill.

If sic a thing should you betide,
To Berwick town to tak a ride,
I'se tak ye up Tweed's bonnie side
      Before ye settle,
And shew you there the fisher's pride,
      A sa'mon-kettle.[2]

---

2 **A sa'mon-kettle**: see Walter Scott, *Guy Mannering* (1815), ch.26, where he writes of a fishing party: "In the meanwhile a liberal distribution of ale and whisky was made among them, besides what was

There lads an' lasses do convene
To feast an' dance upo' the green,
An' there sic brav'ry may be seen
      As will confound ye,
An' gar ye glowr out baith your een
      At a' around ye.

To see sae mony bosoms bare,
An' sic huge puddins i' their hair,
An' some of them wi' naething mair
      Upo' their tete;
Yea, some wi mutches that might scare
      Craws frae their meat.

I ne'er appear'd before in print,
But for your sake would fain be in't,
E'en that I might my wishes hint
      That you'd write mair;
For sure your head-piece is a mint
      Whar wit's nae rare.

Sonse fa me, gif I hadna lure
I could command ilk muse as sure,
Than hae a charot at the door
      To wait upon me;
Tho', poet-like, I'm but a poor
      Mid-Louthian Johnnie.

Berwick, Aug. 31   J.S.

---

called a kettle of fish, – two or three salmon, namely, plunged into a cauldron, and boiled for their supper".

Answer to Mr J.S.'s Epistle

I trou, my mettl'd Louden lathie,[1]
Auld farran birky I maun ca thee,
For whan in gude black print I saw thee
      Wi souple gab,
I skirl'd fou loud, "Oh wae befa thee!
      But thou'rt a daub!"

Awa, ye wylie fleetchin fallow;
The rose shall grow like gowan yallow,
Before I turn sae toom and shallow,
      And void of fusion,
As a' your butter'd words to swallow
      In vain delusion.

Ye mak my Muse a dautit pet,
But gin she could like Allan's mett,[2]
Or couthie cracks and hamely get
      Upon her caritch,[3]
Eithly would I be in your debt
      A pint o' parritch.

At times whan she may lowse her pack,
I'll grant that she can find a knack,

First published in *The Weekly Magazine*, 10 September 1772.

1 **Louden lathie**: here, Fergusson appears to be playing on the dialect of Berwickshire, from where J.S.'s epistle was sent. J.A.H. Murray (later Sir James, first editor of the *Oxford English Dictionary*), in his seminal work *The Dialect of the Southern Counties of Scotland* (London, 1873, p.121) noted of this dialect: "There has been a confusion between *d* and the *voiced th* (dh)" and gave examples of *aether, blaether, laether, fother, uther* for *adder, bladder, ladder, fodder, udder*; and *bodder, fadom, wurdie* for *bother, fathom, worthy*.

2 **mett**: rhyme.

3 **get upon her caritch**: get off by heart (like the catechism).

To gar auld-warld wordies clack
      In hamespun rhyme,
While ilk ane at his billie's back
      Keeps gude Scots time.

But she maun e'en be glad to jook,
And play *teet-bo* frae nook to nook,
Or blush as gin she had the yook
      Upon her skin,
Whan Ramsay or whan Pennicuik[4]
      Their lilts begin.

At morning air,[5] or late at e'en,
Gin ye sud hap to come and see ane,
Not niggard wife, nor greetin wee ane,
      Within my cloyster,
Can challenge you and me frae priein
      A caller oyster.

Heh lad! it would be news indeed,
War I to ride to bonny Tweed,
Wha ne'er laid gamon owr a steed
      Beyont Lusterrick;[6]
And auld shanks' nag would tire, I dreid,
      To pace to Berwick.

You crack weel o' your lasses there,
Their glancin een and bisket[7] bare;

---

4 **Pennicuik**: Alexander Pennecuik (d.1730) was an Edinburgh poet and acquaintance of Allan Ramsay, who wrote humorous, often crude verses, notable for their occasionally sharp social observation.
5 **At morning air**: early in the morning.
6 **Lusterrick**: the old name for the village of Restalrig east of Edinburgh, was Lestalric, after the Barony of that name, which stretched from Leith along the coast to what is now Portobello, and which was owned by the Norman de Lestalric family from the 12th to the 14th century. Fergusson gives the old local pronunciation.
7 **bisket**: i.e. brisket, the breast.

But thof this town be smeekit sair,
      I'll wad a farden,
Than ours they're nane mair fat and fair,
      Cravin your pardon.

Gin heaven should gie the earth a drink,
And afterhend a sunny blink,
Gin ye war here, I'm sure you'd think
      It worth your notice,
To see them dubbs and gutters jink
      Wi kiltit coaties.

And frae ilk corner o' the nation,
We've lasses eke of recreation,
That at close-mouths tak up their station
      By ten o'clock.
The Lord deliver frae temptation
      A' honest fock!

Thir queans are ay upon the catch
For pursie, pocket-book, or watch,
And can sae glibb their leesins hatch,
      That you'll agree,
Ye canna eithly meet their match
      'Tween you and me.

For this gude sample o' your skill,
I'm restin you a pint o' yill,
By and attour a Highland gill
      Of *aqua vitae*;
The which to come and sock[8] at will,
      I here invite ye.

Tho' jillet Fortune scoul and quarrel,
And keep me frae a bien beef barrel,

---

8 **sock**: sink.

As lang's I've twopence i' the warl',
      I'll ay be vockie
To part a fadge or girdle farl
      Wi Louden Jockie.

Farewell, my cock! Lang may ye thrive,
Weel happit in a cozy hive;[9]
And that your saul may never dive
      To Acheron,[10]
I'll wish as lang's I can subscrive
      Rob. Fergusson.

---

9 **hive**: haven.
10 **Acheron**: the "woeful river" of the underworld; by extension, Hades or Hell itself.

Braid Claith

Ye wha are fain to hae your name
Wrote in the bonny book of fame,
Let merit nae pretension claim
    To laurel'd wreath,
But hap ye weel, baith back and wame,
    In gude Braid Claith.

He that some ells o' this may fa,[1]
An' slae-black hat on pow like snaw,
Bids bauld to bear the gree awa,
    Wi a' this graith,
Whan bienly clad wi shell fu braw
    O' gude Braid Claith.

Waesuck for him wha has na feck o't!
For he's a gowk they're sure to geck at,
A chiel that ne'er will be respeckit,
    While he draws breath,
Till his four quarters are bedeckit
    Wi gude Braid Claith.

On Sabbath-days the barber spark,
Whan he has done wi scrapin wark,
Wi siller broachie in his sark,
    Gangs trigly, faith!

First published in *The Weekly Magazine*, 15 October 1772. *The Caledonian Mercury* reprinted it on 12 June 1773, opining that "this poem exhibits so many qualities of true excellence that we quote it entire for our readers, as so many persons of polite taste desired to see it."
1 **fa**: obtain, happen to come by.

Or to the Meadow, or the Park,[2]
    In gude Braid Claith.

Weel might ye trou, to see them there,
That they to shave your haffits bare,
Or curl an' sleek a pickle hair,
    Would be right laith,
Whan pacing wi a gawsy air
    In gude Braid Claith.

If ony mettl'd stirrah grien
For favour frae a lady's een,
He maunna care for being seen
    Before he sheath
His body in a scabbard clean
    O' gude Braid Claith.

For, gin he come wi coat thread-bare,
A feg for him she winna care,
But crook her bonny mou fu sair,
    And scald him baith.
Wooers should ay their travel spare
    Without Braid Claith.

Braid Claith lends fock an unco heeze;
Makes mony kail-worms butter-flees;
Gies mony a doctor his degrees
    For little skaith:
In short, you may be what you please
    Wi gude Braid Claith.

For thof ye had as wise a snout on
As Shakespeare or Sir Isaac Newton,

---

2 **Or to the Meadow, or the Park**: Hope Park (now the Meadows) and the King's Park (enclosing Arthur's Seat and Salisbury Crags) were popular for promenading.

Your judgment fouk would hae a dout on,
    I'll tak my aith,
Till they could see ye wi a suit on
    O' gude Braid Claith.

*A fashionable company promenading
on North Bridge, 1784*

An Eclogue, to the Memory of Dr William Wilkie, Late Professor of Natural Philosophy in the University of St Andrews

GEORDIE
Blaw saft, my reed, and kindly to my mane,
Weel may ye thole a saft and dowie strain;
Nae mair to you shall shepherds in a ring
Wi blythness skip, or lasses lilt an' sing;
Sic sorrow now maun sadden ilka ee,
An' ilka waefu shepherd, grieve wi me.

DAVIE
Wharefor begin a sad an' dowie strain,
Or banish lilting frae the Fifan plain?
Tho' simmer's gane, an' we nae langer view
The blades o' claver wat wi pearls o' dew,
Cauld winter's bleakest blasts we'll eithly cowr,
Our eldin's driven, an' our har'st is owr;
Our rucks fu thick are stackit i' the yeard,
For the Yule-feast a sautit mart's[1] prepar'd;
The ingle-nook supplies the simmer fields,
An' aft as mony gleefu maments yields.
Swyth man! fling a' your sleepy springs awa,
An' on your canty whistle gie's a blaw:
Blythness, I trou, maun lighten ilka ee,
An' ilka canty callant sing like me.

First published in *The Weekly Magazine*, 29 October 1772. Wilkie had taken a liking to the young Fergusson at St Andrews, and would certainly not have discouraged his literary inclinations. He died on 10 October 1772. (See Introduction.) Here, in typical pastoral style, he is referred to familiarly by two shepherds, Geordie and Davie, as one of their own kind.

1 **a sautit mart**: a salted cow or ox fattened and salted for winter consumption.

GEORDIE
Na, na; a canty spring wad now impart
Just threefald sorrow to my heavy heart.
Thof to the weet my ripen'd aits had fawn,
Or shake-winds owr my rigs wi pith had blawn,
To this I could hae said, "I carena by",
Nor fund occasion now my cheeks to dry.
Crosses like thae, or lake o' warld's gear,
Are naething whan we tyne a friend that's dear.
Ah! wae's me for you, Willy! mony a day
Did I wi you on yon broom-thackit brae
Hound aff my sheep, an' lat them careless gang
To harken to your cheery tale or sang;
Sangs that for ay, on Caledonia's strand,
Shall fit the foremost 'mang her tunefu' band.
  I dreamt yestreen his deadly wraith I saw
Gang by my een as white's the driven snaw;
My colley, Ringie, youf'd an' yowl'd a' night,
Cour'd an' crap near me in an unco fright;
I waken'd fley'd, an' shook baith lith an' limb;
A cauldness took me, an' my sight grew dim;
I kent that it forspak approachin wae
When my poor doggie was disturbit sae.
Nae sooner did the day begin to dawn,
Than I beyont the knowe fu speedy ran,
Whare I was keppit wi the heavy tale
That sets ilk dowie sangster to bewail.

DAVIE
An' wha on Fifan bents can weel refuse
To gie the tear o' tribute to his muse? –
Fareweel ilk cheery spring, ilk canty note,
Be daffin an' ilk idle play forgot;
Bring ilka herd the mournfu, mournfu boughs,
Rosemary sad, and ever dreary yews;[2]

---

[2] **Rosemary sad, and ever dreary yews**: rosemary, commonly an

Thae lat be steepit i' the saut, saut tear,
To weet wi hallow'd draps his sacred bier,
Whase sangs will ay in Scotland be rever'd,
While slow-gawn owsen turn the flow'ry swaird;
While bonny lambies lick the dews of spring,
While gaudsmen whistle, or while birdies sing.

GEORDIE
'Twas na for weel tim'd verse or sangs alane,
He bore the bell frae ilka shepherd swain.
Nature to him had gien a kindly lore,
Deep a' her mystic ferlies to explore:
For a' her secret workings he could gie
Reasons that wi her principles agree.
Ye saw yoursel how weel his mailin thrave,
Ay better faugh'd an' snodit than the lave;
Lang had the thristles an' the dockans been
In use to wag their taps upo' the green,
Whare now his bonny rigs delight the view,
An' thrivin hedges drink the caller dew.[3]

DAVIE
They tell me, Geordie, he had sic a gift
That scarce a starnie blinkit frae the lift,
But he would some auld warld name for't find,
As gart him keep it freshly in his mind:
For this some ca'd him an uncanny wight;
The clash gaed round, "he had the second sight",
A tale that never fail'd to be the pride
Of grannies spinnin at the ingle side.

---

emblem of remembrance, and the yew, a symbol of immortality.

3 **An' thrivin hedges drink the caller dew**: Fergusson's own note to this line reads: "Dr Wilkie had a farm near St Andrews, at which he made remarkable improvements." The combination of man of letters and agricultural improver typified the intellectual drive of the Scottish Enlightenment. The succeeding lines spoken by Davie nicely juxtapose popular astonishment, mixed with superstition, at such learning.

GEORDIE
But now he's gane, an' Fame that, whan alive,
Seenil lats ony o' her vot'ries thrive,
Will frae his shinin name a' motes withdraw,
And on her loudest trump his praises blaw.
Lang may his sacred banes untroubl'd rest!
Lang may his truff in gowans gay be drest!
Scholars and bards unheard of yet shall come,
And stamp memorials on his grassy tomb,
Which in yon ancient kirk-yard shall remain,
Fam'd as the urn that hads the Mantuan swain.[4]

---

[4] **the Mantuan swain:** Virgil.

An Eclogue

'Twas e'ening whan the spreckled gowdspink sang,
Whan new-faan dew in blobs o' crystal hang;
Than Will and Sandie thought they'd wrought eneugh,
And loos'd their sair toil'd owsen frae the pleugh:
Before they ca'd their cattle to the town,
The lads to draw their breath e'en sat them down:
To the stiff sturdy aik they lean'd their backs,
While honest Sandie thus began the cracks.

SANDIE
Yence I could hear the laverock's shrill-tun'd throat,
And listen to the clattering gowdspink's note;
Yence I could whistle cantily as they,
To owsen, as they till'd my raggit clay;
But now I would as leive maist lend my lugs
To tuneless puddocks croakin i' the boggs;
I sigh at hame, a-field am dowie too,
To sowf a tune I'll never crook my mou.

WILLIE
Foul fa me[1] gif your bridal had na been
Nae langer bygane than sin Hallow-e'en,
I could hae tell'd you but[2] a warlock's art,
That some daft lightlyin quean had stown your heart;
Our beasties here will take their e'ening pluck,
An' now sin Jock's gane hame the byres to muck,
Fain would I houp my friend will be inclin'd
To gie me a' the secrets o' his mind:
Heh! Sandie, lad, what dool's come owr ye noo,
That you to whistle ne'er will crook your mou?

Published in *Poems* (1773).
1 **Foul fa me**: the devil take me.
2 **but**: without.

SANDIE
Ah! Willie, Willie, I may date my wae
Frae what beted me on my bridal day;
Sair may I rue the hour in which our hands
Were knit thegither in the haly bands;
Sin that I thrave sae ill, in troth I fancy,
Some fiend or fairy, nae sae very chancy,
Has driven me by pauky wiles uncommon,
To wed this flyting fury of a woman.

WILLIE
Ah! Sandie, aften hae I heard you tell,
Amang the lasses a' she bure the bell;
And say, the modest glances o' her een
Far dang the brightest beauties o' the green;
You ca'd her ay sae innocent, sae young,
I thought she kent na how to use her tongue.

SANDIE
Before I married her, I'll take my aith,
Her tongue was never louder than her breath;
But now it's turn'd sae souple and sae bauld,
That Job himsel could scarcely thole the scauld.

WILLIE
Lat her yelp on, be you as calm's a mouse,
Nor lat your whisht be heard into the house;
Do what she can, or be as loud's she please,
Ne'er mind her flytes but set your heart at ease,
Sit down and blaw your pipe, nor faush your thumb,
An' there's my hand she'll tire, and soon sing dumb;
Sooner should winter cald confine the sea,
An' lat the sma'est o' our burns rin free;
Sooner at Yule-day shall the birk be drest,
Or birds in sapless busses bigg their nest,
Before a tonguey woman's noisy plea
Should ever be a cause to danton me.

SANDIE
Weel could I this abide, but oh! I fear
I'll soon be twin'd o' a' my warldly gear;
My kirnstaff now stands gizzen'd at the door,
My cheese-rack toom that ne'er was toom before;
My kye may now rin rowtin to the hill,
And on the nakit yird their milkness spill;
She seenil lays her hand upon a turn,
Neglects the kebbuck, and forgets the kirn;
I vow my hair-mould milk would poison dogs,
As it stands lapper'd in the dirty cogs.
 Before the seed I sell'd my ferra coo,[3]
An' wi the profit coft a stane o' woo:
I thought, by priggin, that she might hae spun
A plaidie, light, to screen me frae the sun;
But though the siller's scant, the cleedin dear,
She has na ca'd about a wheel the year.
Last ouk but ane I was frae hame a day,
Buying a threave or twa o' bedding strae:
O' ilka thing the woman had her will,
Had fouth o' meal to bake, and hens to kill:
But hyn awa to Edinbrough scoured she
To get a making o' her fav'rite tea:
And 'cause I left her not the weary clink,
She sellt the very trunchers frae my bink.

WILLIE
Her tea! ah! wae betide sic costly gear,
Or them that ever wad the price o't spier.
Sin my auld gutcher first the warld knew,
Fouk had na fund the Indies, whare it grew.
I mind mysel, it's nae sae lang sin syne,
Whan Auntie Marion did her stamack tyne,

---

3 **ferra coo**: farrow cow, i.e. one without a calf, not giving milk.

That Davs our gardiner came frae Apple-bogg,[4]
An' gae her tea[5] to tak by way o' drog.

SANDIE
Whan ilka herd for cauld his fingers rubs,
An' cakes o' ice are seen upo' the dubbs;
At morning, whan frae pleugh or fauld I come,
I'll see a braw reik rising frae my lum,
An' ablins think to get a rantin blaze
To fley the frost awa an' toast my taes;
But whan I shoot my nose in, ten to ane
If I weelfardly see my ain hearthstane;
She round the ingle with her gimmers sits,
Crammin their gabbies wi her nicest bits,
While the gudeman outby maun fill his crap
Frae the milk cogie, or the parritch cap.

WILLIE
Sandie, gif this were ony common plea,
I should the lealest o' my counsel gie;
But mak or meddle betwixt man and wife,
Is what I never did in a' my life.
It's wearin on now to the tail o' May,
An' just between the bear seed and the hay;
As lang's an orra morning may be spar'd,
Stap your wa's[6] east the haugh, an' tell the laird;

---

4 **Apple-bogg**: apparently a place-name invented by Fergusson.
5 **tea**: still an expensive item, although scarcely an innovation as it had been used in Scotland for more than fifty years. It was nevertheless much frowned upon by old-fashioned folk. In the 1790s the minister of Crieff Robert Stirling commented: "About 20 times more tea is used now than 20 years ago. Bewitched by the mollifying influence of an enfeebling potion, the very poorest classes begin to regard it as one of the necessaries of life, and for its sake resign the cheaper and more invigorating nourishment which the productions of their country afford."(*Statistical Account of Scotland*, 1793, Vol.9, p.594, footnote)
6 **Stap your wa's**: step your way.

For he's a man weel vers'd in a' the laws,
Kens baith their outs and ins, their cracks and flaws,
An' ay right gleg, whan things are out o' joint,
At sattlin o' a nice or kittle point.
But yonder's Jock, he'll ca your owsen hame,
And tak thir tidings to your thrawart dame,
That ye're awa ae peacefu meal to prie,
And take your supper kail or sowens wi me.

Hallow-Fair

At Hallowmas, whan nights grow lang,
    And starnies shine fu clear,
Whan fock, the nippin cald to bang,
    Their winter hap-warms wear,
Near Edinbrough[1] a fair there hads,
    I wat there's nane whase name is,
For strappin dames and sturdy lads,
    And cap and stoup, mair famous
                Than it that day.

Upo' the tap o' ilka lum
    The sun began to keek,
And bade the trig-made maidens come
    A sightly joe to seek
At Hallow-fair, whare browsters rare
    Keep gude ale on the gantries,
And dinna scrimp ye o' a skair
    O' kebbucks frae their pantries,
                Fu saut that day.

Here country John in bonnet blue,
    An' eke his Sunday's claes on,
Rins after Meg wi rokelay new,
    An' sappy kisses lays on;
She'll tauntin say, "Ye silly coof!
    Be o' your gab mair sparin."
He'll tak the hint, and criesh her loof
    Wi what will buy her fairin,
                To chow that day.

First published in *The Weekly Magazine*, 12 November 1772. The fair was held at Hallowmas, in the first week of November.
1 **Near Edinbrough**: the fair was held at Castle Barns, west of the town near what is now Fountainbridge.

Here chapmen billies tak their stand,
   An' shaw their bonny wallies;
Wow, but they lie fu gleg aff hand
   To trick the silly fallows;
Heh, sirs! what cairds and tinklers come,
   An' ne'er-do-weel horse-coupers,
An' spae-wives fenzying to be dumb,
   Wi a' siclike landloupers,
            To thrive that day.

Here Sawny cries, frae Aberdeen,[2]
   "Come ye to me fa need;
The brawest shanks that e'er were seen
   I'll sell ye cheap an' gweed.
I wyt they are as protty hose
   As come frae weyr or leem:
Here tak a rug and shaw's your pose;[3]
   Forseeth, my ain's but teem
            An' light this day."

Ye wives, as ye gang thro' the fair,
   O mak your bargains hooly!
O' a' thir wylie louns beware,
   Or fegs! they will ye spulzie.
For fairn-year Meg Thamson got,
   Frae thir mischievous villains,
A scaw'd bit o' a penny note,
   That lost a score o' shillins
            To her that day.

The dinlin drums alarm our ears,
   The serjeant screechs fu loud,

---

[2] **frae Aberdeen**: Fergusson's parents were from Aberdeenshire, and he had spent six months at his uncle's farm near Old Meldrum in 1769, so was very familiar with the distinctive dialect that he imitates here.

[3] **Here tak a rug and shaw's your pose**: here, get yourself a bargain, and let's see your store of money.

"A' gentlemen and volunteers
   That wish your country gude,
Come here to me, and I sall gie
   Twa guineas and a croun,
A bowl o' punch, that like the sea
   Will soum a lang dragoon
                 Wi ease this day."

Without, the cuissers prance and nicker,
   An' owr the ley-rig scud;
In tents the carles bend the bicker,
   An' rant an' roar like wud.
Then there's sic yellochin and din,
   Wi wives and wee-anes gabblin,
That ane might trou they were akin
   To a' the tongues at Babylon,
                 Confus'd that day.

Whan Phoebus ligs in Thetis' lap,[4]
   Auld Reikie gies them shelter,
Whare cadgily they kiss the cap,
   An' ca't round helter-skelter.
Jock Bell gaed furth to play his freaks,
   Great cause he had to rue it,
For frae a stark Lochaber aix
   He gat a clamihewit,
                 Fu sair that night.

"Ohon!" quo he, "I'd rather be
   By sword or bagnet stickit,

---

4 **Whan Phoebus ligs in Thetis' lap**: in Greek mythology, Thetis was the chief of the Nereids, or sea-nymphs, the fifty daughters of Nereus, the old man of the sea. Hence, "when the sun lies in the sea's lap". Strictly speaking, this is not an accurate description of night falling on Edinburgh, but since, depending on one's viewing-point, the sun does rise over the sea it could be said to spend the hours of darkness in its embrace.

Than hae my crown or body wi
    Sic deadly weapons nickit."
Wi that he gat anither straik,
    Mair weighty than before,
That gar'd his feckless body aik,
    An' spew the reikin gore,
            Fu red that night.

He peching on the cawsey lay,
    O' kicks and cuffs weel sair'd;
A Highland aith the serjeant gae,
    "She maun pe see our guard."⁵
Out spak the weirlike corporal,
    "Pring in ta drunken sot."
They trail'd him ben, an' by my saul
    He paid his drunken groat
            For that neist day.

Good fock, as ye come frae the fair,
    Bide yont frae this black squad;
There's nae sic savages elsewhere
    Allow'd to wear cockade.
Than the strong lion's hungry maw,
    Or tusk o' Russian bear,
Frae their wanruly fellin paw
    Mair cause ye hae to fear
            Your death that day.

A wee soup drink dis unco weel
    To had the heart aboon;
It's good as lang's a canny chiel
    Can stand steeve in his shoon.

---

5 **She maun pe see our guard**: see note to 'The Daft-Days'. Fergusson is mocking the Highland accents of the City Guard. "Guard" should be pronounced *Guaird* throughout.

But gin a birkie's owr weel sair'd,
   It gars him aften stammer
To pleys that bring him to the guard,
   An' eke the Council-chawmir,
               Wi shame that day.

Three Captains of the City Guard, 1786

The Lee-Rigg

Will ye gang owr the lee-rigg,
   My ain kind deary O!
And cuddle there sae kindly
   Wi me, my kind deary O?

At thornie-dike and birken-tree
   We'll daff, and ne'er be weary O;
They'll scug ill een frae you and me,
   Mine ain kind deary O.

Nae herds wi kent or colly there,
   Shall ever come to fear ye O;
But lav'rocks, whistling in the air,
   Shall woo, like me, their deary O!

While others herd their lambs and ewes,
   And toil for warld's gear, my jo,
Upon the lee my pleasure grows,
   Wi you, my kind dearie O!

First published in *The Charmer: A Collection of Songs... Vol II. An entire New Collection* (Edinburgh, 1782). It then appeared under the title 'My ain kind dearie O' in the first volume of James Johnson's *Scots Musical Museum* (1787). In a note on this Robert Burns wrote: "The old words of this song are omitted here, though much more beautiful than these inserted; which were mostly composed by poor Ferguson [sic], in one of his merry humours." The song, of course, is the basis for Burns's own 'The Lea-Rig'.

To The Tron-Kirk Bell

Wanwordy, crazy, dinsome thing,
As e'er was fram'd to jow or ring,
What gar'd them sic in steeple hing,
    They ken themsel,
But weel wat I they couldna bring
    Waur sounds frae hell.

What deil are ye? that I shud ban,
You're neither kin to pat nor pan;
Not ulie pig, nor maister-cann,
    But weel may gie
Mair pleasure to the ear o' man
    Than stroak o' thee.

Fleece merchants may look bald,[1] I trou,
Sin a' Auld Reikie's childer noo
Maun stap their lugs wi teats o' woo,
    Thy sound to bang,
And keep it frae gawn thro' and thro',
    Wi jarrin twang.

Your noisy tongue, there's nae abidin't,
Like scaulding wife's, there is nae guidin't;
Whan I'm 'bout ony bus'ness eident,
    It's sair to thole;

    First published in *The Weekly Magazine*, 26 November 1772. The Tron Kirk stands at the junction of the High Street and the Bridges, and is named after the salt-tron, or weighing-beam, which formerly stood at the site. The kirk was built between 1637 and 1663, and the bell was put in in 1673. It seems that after a hundred years the bell was worn out and cracked ("wanwordy, crazy" means "worthless, damaged"), hence Fergusson's complaint. In August 1774 the Dean of Guild ordered that it be sent to London and a new bell bought there.
1 **bald**: i.e. bold, but also a pun on baldness.

To deave me, than, ye tak a pride in't
    Wi senseless knoll.

O! war I provost o' the toun,
I swear by a' the pow'rs aboon,
I'd bring ye wi a reesle doun;
    Nor shud you think
(Sae sair I'd crack and clour your croun)
    Again to clink.

For whan I've toom'd the muckle cap,
An' fain wud fa owr in a nap,
Troth I cud doze as sound's a tap,
    Wer't na for thee,
That gies the tither weary chap
    To wauken me.

I dreamt ae night I saw Auld Nick;
Quo he, "This bell o' mine's a trick,
A wylie piece o' politic,
    A cunnin snare
To trap fock in a cloven stick,
    Ere they're aware.

"As lang's my dautit bell hings there,
A'body at the kirk will skair;
Quo they, 'Gif he that preaches there
    Like it can wound,
We downa care a single hair
    For joyfu sound.'"[2]

---

[2] There are two possible interpretations of the Devil's logic: either that, as long as his beloved bell hangs there, everybody will take fright ("skair") at the kirk and stay away; or that, everybody who goes to the kirk will share ("skair") its "antimelody" and as a result be in constant misery. The irony of the succeeding stanza ("sic honest folk") would suggest the second interpretation.

If magistrates wi me wud 'gree,
For ay tongue-tackit shud you be,
Nor fleg wi antimelody
      Sic honest fock,
Whase lugs were never made to dree
      Thy doolfu shock.

But far frae thee the bailies dwell,
Or they wud scunner at your knell:
Gie the foul thief[3] his riven bell,
      And than, I trou,
The byword hads, "The deil himsel
      Has got his due."

---

3 **the foul thief:** the Devil.

Caller Water

Whan father Adie first pat spade in
The bonny yeard of ancient Eden,
His amry had nae liquor laid in
    To fire his mou,
Nor did he thole his wife's upbraidin
    For being fou.

A caller burn o' siller sheen
Ran cannily out owr the green,
And whan our gutcher's drouth had been
    To bide right sair,
He loutit down and drank bedeen
    A dainty skair.

His bairns a' before the flood
Had langer tack o' flesh and blood,
And on mair pithy shanks they stood
    Than Noah's line,
Wha still hae been a feckless brood
    Wi drinking wine.

The fuddlin bardies now-a-days
Rin maukin-mad in Bacchus' praise,
And limp and stoiter thro' their lays
    Anacreontic,[1]
While each his sea of wine displays,
    As big's the Pontic.

First published in *The Weekly Magazine*, 21 January 1773.
1 **Anacreontic:** a type of verse of the kind composed by the Greek poet Anacreon (born c.570 BC), who wrote lyrics in praise of wine. Bacchus of course was the Roman god of wine.

My muse will no gang far frae hame,
Or scour a' airths to hound for fame;
In troth, the jillet ye might blame
    For thinking on't,
Whan eithly she can find the theme
    Of *aqua font*.

This is the name that doctors use
Their patients' noddles to confuse;
Wi simples clad in terms abstruse,
    They labour still,
In kittle words to gar you roose
    Their want o' skill.

But we'll hae nae sic clitter-clatter,
And briefly to expound the matter
It shall be ca'd good *Caller Water*,
    Than whilk, I trou,
Few drogs in doctors' shops are better
    For me or you.

Tho' joints are stiff as ony rung,
Your pith wi pain be fairly dung,
Be you in Caller Water flung
    Out owr the lugs,
'Twill mak you souple, swack and young,
    Withouten drugs.

Tho' cholic or the heart-scad teaze us,
Or ony inward pain should seize us,
It masters a' sic fell diseases
    That would ye spulzie,
And brings them to a canny crisis,
    Wi little tulzie.

Wer't na for it the bonny lasses
Would glowr nae mair in keeking glasses,

And soon tyne dint o' a' the graces
      That aft convene
In gleefu looks and bonny faces,
      To catch our een.

The fairest then might die a maid,
And Cupid quit his shooting trade,
For wha thro' clarty masquerade
      Could than discover
Whether the features under shade
      Were worth a lover?

As simmer rains bring simmer flow'rs,[2]
And leaves to cleed the birken bow'rs,
Sae beauty gets, by caller show'rs,
      Sae rich a bloom
As for estate, or heavy dow'rs
      Aft stands in room.

What makes Auld Reikie's dames sae fair?
It canna be the halesome air
But *caller burn* beyond compare,
      The best of ony,
That gars them a' sic graces skair,
      And blink sae bonny.

On May-day[3] in a fairy ring,
We've seen them round St Anthon's spring,
Frae grass the caller dew draps wring
      To weet their een,

---

2 **flow'rs**: the original text has *show'rs* but this is surely a printer's error. Later editions alter it as here.

3 **May-day**: the tradition of girls going to wash their faces in the dew on Arthur's Seat on 1st May still survives. St Anthony's spring is a well on the north side, beside the ruined chapel of the same name.

And water clear as crystal spring,
    To synd them clean.

O may they still pursue the way
To look sae feat, sae clean, sae gay!
Then shall their beauties glance like May,
    And, like her, be
The goddess of the vocal spray,
    The Muse, and me.

Auld Reikie

Auld Reikie, wale o' ilka toun
That Scotland kens beneath the moon;
Whare couthy chiels at e'ening meet
Their bizzing craigs and mous to weet;
And blythly gar auld Care gae by
Wi blinkit and wi bleering eye:
Owr lang frae thee the Muse has been
Sae frisky on the simmer's green,
Whan flowers and gowans wont to glent
In bonny blinks upo' the bent;
But now the leaves a yellow dye,
Peel'd frae the branches, quickly fly;
And now frae nouther bush nor brier
The spreckl'd mavis greets your ear;
Nor bonny blackbird skims and roves
To seek his love in yonder groves.

Then, Reikie, welcome! Thou canst charm
Unfleggit by the year's alarm;

First published separately as *AULD REIKIE, A POEM, By R. FERGUSSON. EDINBURGH: Printed for the AUTHOR; and Sold at OSSIAN'S Head. MDCCLXXIII. [Price SIX PENCE.]* This now extremely rare edition (a copy exists in the British Museum and another at Harvard University) does not contain the last 40 lines, which appeared first in the 1779 Part II edition of Fergusson's *Poems*. The text is followed by the words "END OF CANTO I", and it is clear that Fergusson intended this to be his great work, a "full-length comedy of Edinburgh life. For want of encouragement the undertaking was discontinued." (Matthew P. McDiarmid, *The Poems of Robert Fergusson*, Scottish Text Society, Vol.I, 1954, p.40.) McDiarmid deduces from the opening farewell to summer and description of autumn that its composition was begun late in 1772. It was not included in the 1773 *Poems*, published in early January, but must have appeared very soon after.

Not Boreas, that sae snelly blows,
Dare here pap in his angry nose:
Thanks to our dads, whase biggin stands
A shelter to surrounding lands.[1]

  Now morn, with bonny purpie-smiles,
Kisses the air-cock o' St Giles;
Rakin their een, the servant lasses
Early begin their lies and clashes;
Ilk tells her friend o' saddest distress,
That still she brooks frae scouling mistress;
And wi her joe in turnpike stair
She'd rather snuff the stinking air,
As be subjected to her tongue,
When justly censur'd in the wrong.

  On stair wi tub, or pat in hand,
The barefoot housemaids loo to stand,
That antrin fock may ken how snell
Auld Reikie will at morning smell:
Then, with an inundation big as
The burn that 'neath the Nore Loch Brig is,[2]
They kindly shower Edina's roses,[3]

---

[1] **lands**: tenements.
[2] **Nore Loch Brig**: the Nor' Loch, an unhealthy swamp originally created in 1460 as the city's northern defence, occupied what is now Princes Street Gardens and Waverley Station. It was drained at its eastern end in 1763, and that year Provost George Drummond laid the foundation stone for the North Bridge, the primary link for extending Edinburgh northwards and building the New Town. But the bridge was partially founded on moved earth and in August 1769, only eight months after traffic first began to use it, it collapsed, killing five people. From lines near the end of the poem, it appears that the bridge had not yet been restored while Fergusson was writing 'Auld Reikie', although it was partially back in use by February 1773.
[3] **Edina's roses**: the "flouers o' Edinburgh" or the contents of chamber-pots etc., which were emptied daily into the streets.

To quicken and regale our noses.
Now some for this, wi satire's leesh,
Hae gien auld Edinburgh a creesh:
But without souring nocht is sweet;
The morning smells that hail our street
Prepare, and gently lead the way
To simmer canty, braw and gay;
Edina's sons mair eithly share
Her spices and her dainties rare,
Than he that's never yet been call'd
Aff frae his plaidie or his fauld.

Now stairhead critics, senseless fools,
Censure their aim, and pride their rules,
In Luckenbooths,[4] wi glowring eye,
Their neighbours' sma'est faults descry:
If ony loun should dander there,
Of aukward gate and foreign air,
They trace his steps, till they can tell
His pedigree as weel's himsel.

Whan Phoebus blinks wi warmer ray,
And schools at noonday get the play,
Then bus'ness, weighty bus'ness comes;
The trader glowrs, he doubts, he hums;
The lawyers eke to Cross repair,
Their wigs to shaw, and toss an air;
While busy agent closely plies,
And a' his kittle cases tries.

Now Night, that's cunzied chief for fun,
Is wi her usual rites begun;

---

4 **Luckenbooths**: a collection of enclosed (lucken) booths or shops which lined the High Street opposite St Giles; some even occupied the middle of the street. This early example of a shopping centre (they were first constructed in the 1440s) was demolished finally in 1817.

Thro' ilka gate the torches blaze,
And globes send out their blinking rays.
The usefu cadie⁵ plies in street,
To bide the profits o' his feet;
For by thir lads Auld Reikie's fock
Ken but a sample o' the stock
O' thieves, that nightly wad oppress,
And make baith goods and gear the less.
Near him the lazy chairman stands,
And wats na how to turn his hands,
Till some daft birky, ranting fu,
Has matters somewhere else to do;
The chairman willing gies his light
To deeds o' darkness and o' night:
It's never sax pence for a lift
That gars thir lads wi fu'ness rift;
For they wi better gear are paid,
And whores and culls support their trade.

   Near some lamp-post, wi dowy face,
Wi heavy een and sour grimace,
Stands she that beauty lang had kend,
Whoredom her trade, and vice her end.
But see wharenow she wuns her breid
By that which Nature ne'er decreed,
And sings sad music to the lugs,
'Mang bourachs o' damn'd whores and rogues.
Whane'er we reputation loss,
Fair chastity's transparent gloss,
Redemption seenil kens the name,
But a's black misery and shame.

---

5 **the usefu cadie**: from the French *cadet*. The cadies or caddies were a body of messengers, formally constituted, and regulated by the Council, who would run errands for a small fee. As Fergusson goes on to point out, their profession made them streetwise, and they could supply intelligence regarding many of the city's thieves and petty criminals.

Frae joyous tavern, reeling drunk,
　Wi fiery phizz and een half sunk,
　Behad the bruiser, fae to a'
　That in the reek o' gardies fa:⁶
　Close by his side, a feckless race
　O' macaronies shew their face,
　And think they're free frae skaith or harm,
　While pith befriends their leader's arm:
　Yet fearfu aften o' their maught,
　They quat the glory o' the faught
　To this same warrior wha led
　Thae heroes to bright honour's bed;
　And aft the hack o' honour shines
　In bruiser's face wi broken lines:
　Of them sad tales he tells anon,
　Whan ramble and whan fighting's done;
　And, like Hectorian, ne'er impairs
　The brag and glory o' his sairs.

　　Whan feet in dirty gutters plash,
　And fock to wale their fitstaps fash,
　At night the macaroni drunk,
　In pools or gutters aftimes sunk:
　Hegh! what a fright he now appears,
　Whan he his corpse dejected rears!
　Look at that head, and think if there
　The pomet slaister'd up his hair!
　The cheeks observe, where now could shine
　The scancing glories o' carmine?
　Ah, legs! in vain the silk-worm there
　Display'd to view her eident care;
　For stink, instead of perfumes, grow,
　And clarty odours fragrant flow.

---

6 **fae to a' that in the reek o' gardies fa**: foe to all that come within reach of his raised fists.

Now some to porter, some to punch,
Some to their wife, and some their wench,
Retire, while noisy ten-hours' drum[7]
Gars a' your trades gae dandring home.
Now mony a club, jocose and free,
Gie a' to merriment and glee;
Wi sang and glass they fley the pow'r
O' Care that wad harass the hour:
For wine and Bacchus still bear down
Our thrawart fortune's wildest frown:
It maks you stark, and bauld, and brave,
Ev'n whan descending to the grave.

Now some, in Pandemonium's[8] shade,
Resume the gormandizing trade;
Whare eager looks and glancing een
Forespeak a heart and stamack keen.
Gang on, my lads: it's lang sin syne
We kent auld Epicurus' line;[9]
Save you, the board wad cease to rise,
Bedight wi daintiths to the skies;
And salamanders[10] cease to swill
The comforts of a burning gill.

But chief, O Cape,[11] we crave thy aid,
To get our cares and poortith laid:

---

7   **ten-hours' drum**: in a footnote to his verse-epistle of 10 July 1719, answering William Hamilton's of 26 June, Allan Ramsay writes: "Ten a Clock at Night, when the Drum goes round to warn sober Folks to call for a Bill."
8   **Pandemonium**: a club, also known as the Gormandizing Club.
9   **auld Epicurus' line**: the Greek philosopher (c.341–c.270 BC) taught that pleasure was the highest aim of mankind, but that it should be a pleasure based on sound moral principles leading to physical and spiritual contentment. The latter proviso is usually forgotten by those in pursuit of epicurean delights.
10 **salamanders**: possibly another club.
11 **Cape**: Fergusson was admitted as a member or Knight Companion of the Cape Club on 10 October 1772, styling himself Sir Precenter. (See Introduction.)

Sincerity, and genius true,
Of Knights have ever been the due:
Mirth, music, porter deepest dy'd,
Are never here to worth deny'd;
And health, o' happiness the queen,
Blinks bonny, wi her smile serene.

Tho' joy maist part Auld Reikie owns,
Eftsoons she kens sad sorrow's frowns:
What group is yon sae dismal, grim,
Wi horrid aspect, cleeding dim?
Says Death, "They're mine, a dowy crew,
To me they'll quickly pay their last adieu."

How come mankind, whan lacking woe,
In saulie's face[12] their heart to show,
As if they were a clock, to tell
That grief in them had rung her bell?
Then, what is man? why a' this phrase?[13]
Life's spunk decay'd nae mair can blaze.
Let sober grief alone declare
Our fond anxiety and care:
Nor let the undertakers be
The only waefu friends we see.

Come on, my Muse, and then rehearse
The gloomiest theme in a' your verse:
In morning, whan ane keeks about,
Fu blyth and free frae ail, nae doubt
He lippens not to be misled
Amang the regions of the dead;
But straight a painted corp he sees,
Lang streekit 'neath its canopies.

---

12 **In saulie's face**: a saulie was a hired mourner at a funeral, who preceded the coffin, wearing black and a suitably woeful expression.
13 **why a' this phrase?**: why all this insincerity, effusive talk?

Soon, soon will this his mirth controul,
And send damnation to his soul;
Or when the dead-deal (awful shape!)
Makes frighted mankind girn and gape,
Reflection then his reason sours,
For the neist dead-deal may be ours.
Whan Sybil led the Trojan down[14]
To haggard Pluto's dreary town,
Shapes waur nor thae, I freely ween,
Could never meet the soldier's een.

   If kail sae green, or herbs, delight,
Edina's street attracts the sight;
Not Covent-garden, clad sae braw,
Mair fouth o' herbs can eithly shaw:
For mony a yeard is here sair sought,
That kail and cabbage may be bought,
And healthfu sallad to regale,
Whan pamper'd wi a heavy meal.
Glowr up the street in simmer morn,
The birks sae green, and sweet brier-thorn,
Wi spraingit flow'rs that scent the gale,
Ca far awa the morning smell,
Wi which our ladies flow'r-pats fill'd,
And every noxious vapour kill'd.
O Nature! canty, blyth and free,
Whare is there keeking-glass like thee?
Is there on earth that can compare
Wi Mary's shape, and Mary's air,
Save the empurpl'd speck, that grows
In the saft faulds of yonder rose?
How bonny seems the virgin breast,

---

14 **Whan Sybil led the Trojan down**: Sybil is a corrupt spelling of Sibyl. The sibyls were prophetesses in Roman mythology, and one, Amalthea, accompanied Aeneas on his journey to the underworld, Pluto's kingdom.

Whan by the lilies here caress'd,
And leaves the mind in doubt to tell
Which maist in sweets and hue excel!

    Gillespie's snuff[15] should prime the nose
Of her that to the market[16] goes,
If she wad like to shun the smells
That buoy up frae mirkest cells;
Whare wames o' paunches' sav'ry scent
To nostrils gie great discontent.
Now wha in Albion could expect
O' cleanliness sic great neglect?
Nae Hottentot that daily lairs
'Mang tripe, or ither clarty wares,
Hath ever yet conceiv'd, or seen
Beyond the Line,[17] sic scenes unclean.

    On Sunday here, an alter'd scene
O' men and manners meets our een:
Ane wad maist trou some people chose
To change their faces wi their clo'es,
And fain wad gar ilk neighbour think
They thirst for goodness as for drink;
But there's an unco dearth o' grace,
That has nae mansion but the face,
And never can obtain a part
In benmost corner o' the heart.
Why should religion make us sad,
If good frae virtue's to be had?
Na, rather gleefu turn your face;
Forsake hypocrisy, grimace;

---

15 **Gillespie's snuff**: John and James Gillespie's snuff and tobacco shop was on the north side of the High Street. James (1726–97) left his fortune to found a hospital and a school.
16 **market**: the Fleshmarket, situated off the High Street just west of North Bridge, in present-day Fleshmarket Close.
17 **the Line**: the equator.

And never have it understood
You fleg mankind frae being good.

In afternoon, a' brawly buskit,
The joes and lasses loo to frisk it:
Some tak a great delight to place
The modest *bon-grace* owr the face;
Tho' you may see, if so inclin'd,
The turning o' the leg behind.
Now Comely-Garden, and the Park,[18]
Refresh them after forenoon's wark;
Newhaven, Leith, or Canon-mills,[19]
Supply them in their Sunday's gills,
Whare writers aften spend their pence,
To stock their heads wi drink and sense.

While dand'ring cits delight to stray
To Castlehill, or public way,
Whare they nae other purpose mean
Than that fool cause o' being seen;
Let me to Arthur's Seat pursue,
Whare bonny pastures meet the view,
And mony a wild-lorn scene accrues,
Befitting Willie Shakespeare's muse:
If Fancy there would join the thrang,
The desert rocks and hills amang,
To echoes we should lilt and play,
And gie to mirth the lee-lang day.

Or should some canker'd biting shour
The day and a' her sweets deflour,
To Holy-rood-house let me stray,
And gie to musing a' the day;

---

18 **Comely-Garden, and the Park**: public gardens east of Holyrood, in the Abbeyhill area, and the King's Park.
19 **Canon-mills**: then a village north of the city.

Lamenting what auld Scotland knew,
Bien days for ever frae her view:
O Hamilton, for shame![20] the Muse
Would pay to thee her couthy vows,
Gin ye wad tent the humble strain,
And gie's our dignity again;
For O, wae's me! the thistle springs
In domicile of ancient kings,
Without a patriot to regret
Our palace and our ancient state.

   Blest place! whare debtors daily run,[21]
To rid themselves frae jail and dun;
Here, tho' sequester'd frae the din
That rings Auld Reikie's waas within,
Yet they may tread the sunny braes,
And brook Apollo's cheery rays;
Glowr frae St Anthon's grassy hight,
Owr vales in simmer claes bedight,
Nor ever hing their head, I ween,
Wi jealous fear o' being seen.
May I, whanever duns come nigh,
And shake my garret wi their cry,
Scour here wi haste, protection get,
To screen mysel frae them and debt;

---

20 **O Hamilton, for shame!:** the Duke of Hamilton, the hereditary keeper of Holyrood Palace, lived in part of it, but most of the building was in a derelict state. There had been no royal function there since Charles I's coronation in 1633, apart from Prince Charles Edward Stewart's use of it for his court in 1745 – which in itself had tainted it as far as the authorities were concerned and no doubt encouraged its neglect. Fergusson, as a staunch patriot, viewed the state of the palace as a national disgrace.
21 **whare debtors daily run:** debtors could claim the right of sanctuary within the precincts of Holyrood Abbey, next to the palace. This safe zone included the whole of the King's Park.

To breathe the bliss of open sky,
And Simon Fraser's[22] bolts defy.

Now gin a loun should hae his claes
In thread-bare autumn o' their days,
St Mary,[23] brokers' guardian saint,
Will satisfy ilk ail and want;
For mony a hungry writer there
Dives down at night, wi cleeding bare,
And quickly rises to the view
A gentleman, perfite and new.
Ye rich fock, look no wi disdain
Upo' this ancient Brokage Lane!
For naked poets are supplied
With what you to their wants deny'd.

Peace to thy shade, thou wale o' men,
Drummond![24] relief to poortith's pain:
To thee the greatest bliss we owe,
And tribute's tear shall grateful flow:
The sick are cur'd, the hungry fed,
And dreams of comfort tend their bed:
As lang as Forth weets Lothian's shore,
As lang's on Fife her billows roar,
Sae lang shall ilk whase country's dear,
To thy remembrance gie a tear.
By thee Auld Reikie thrave, and grew

---

22 **Simon Fraser**: then keeper of the Tolbooth prison.
23 **St Mary**: in William & Robert Chambers' 1840 edition of *The Poetical Works of Robert Fergusson*, it is noted: "St Mary's Wynd is a mean street in Edinburgh, exclusively occupied by dealers in old clothes."
24 **Drummond**: George Drummond (1687–1766) was six times Lord Provost and was the political driving force behind the modernisation of Edinburgh. A social improver, he raised funds to establish the Infirmary, established five medical Chairs at the University, and was responsible for the construction of North Bridge and the plans for the New Town.

Delightfu to her childer's view:
Nae mair shall Glasgow striplings threap
Their city's beauty and its shape,
While our new city spreads around
Her bonny wings on fairy ground.

   But provosts now that ne'er afford
The sma'est dignity to *lord*,[25]
Ne'er care tho' ev'ry scheme gae wild
That Drummond's sacred hand has cull'd:
The spacious Brig neglected lies,
Tho' plagued wi pamphlets, dunn'd wi cries;
They heed not tho' destruction come
To gulp us in her gaunting womb.
O shame! that safety canna claim
Protection from a provost's name,
But hidden danger lies behind
To torture and to fleg the mind;
I may as weel bid Arthur's Seat
To Berwick-Law make gleg retreat,
As think that either will or art
Shall get the gate to win their heart;
For *politics* are a' their mark,
Bribes latent, and corruption dark:
If they can eithly turn the pence,
Wi city's good they will dispense;
Nor care tho' a' her sons were lair'd
Ten fathom i' the auld kirk-yeard.

   To sing yet meikle does remain,
Undecent for a modest strain;
And since the poet's daily bread is
The favour of the Muse or ladies,

---

25 **lord**: i.e. provosts since Drummond give no dignity to the title *Lord* Provost.

He downa like to gie offence
To delicacy's bonny sense;
Therefore the stews remain unsung,
And bawds in silence drop their tongue.

   Reikie, fareweel! I ne'er could part
Wi thee but wi a dowy heart.
Aft frae the Fifan coast I've seen
Thee tow'ring on thy summit green;
So glowr the saints when first is given
A fav'rite keek o' glore and heaven:
On earth nae mair they bend their een,
But quick assume angelic mien;
So I on Fife wad glowr no more,
But gallop'd to Edina's shore.

Mutual Complaint of Plainstanes and Causey, in their Mother-tongue

Since Merlin[1] laid Auld Reikie's causey,
And made her o' his wark right saucy,
The spacious *street* and *plainstanes*
Were never kend to crack but anes,
Whilk happened on the hinder night,
Whan Fraser's ulie[2] tint its light;
Of Highland sentries nane were waukin,
To hear thir cronies glibly talkin;
For them this wonder might hae rotten,
And, like night robb'ry, been forgotten,
Had na a cadie, wi his lanthron,
Been gleg enough to hear them bant'rin,
Wha came to me neist morning early,
To gie me tidings o' this ferly.
 Ye taunting louns trou this nae joke,
For anes the ass of Balaam[3] spoke,
Better than lawyers do, forsooth,
For it spake naething but the truth:
Whether they follow its example,
You'll ken best whan you hear the sample.

 First published in *The Weekly Magazine*, 4 March 1773. *Plainstanes* is the pavement, *Causey* the causeway or street. The poem clearly influenced Burns's 'The Brigs of Ayr'.
1 **Merlin**: by tradition, a Frenchman named John Marlin or Merlioun first paved the High Street of Edinburgh. This may or may not be the same "French paviour" as John Mayser, who with Bartilme Foliot was contracted by the Common Council to undertake such work in 1532. The 16th-century Marlin's Wynd was named after him (its remnants were excavated within the Tron Kirk in 1974) and he is reputed to have been buried beneath the street with the spot marked by six flat stones laid in the shape of a coffin.
2 **Fraser's ulie**: Fraser was the contractor for the city's oil-lamps.
3 **the ass of Balaam**: see the Bible, Numbers, ch.xxii.

PLAINSTANES
My friend, thir hunder years and mair,
We've been forfoughen late and air,
In sunshine, and in weety weather,
Our thrawart lot we bure thegither.
I never growl'd, but was content
Whan ilk ane had an equal stent,
But now to flyte I'se e'en be bauld,
Whan I'm wi sic a grievance thrall'd.
How haps it, say, that mealy bakers,
Hair-kaimers, crieshy gezy-makers,
Should a' get leave to waste their powders
Upon my beaux and ladies' shoulders?
My travellers are fley'd to deid
Wi creels wanchancy, heap'd wi breid,
Frae whilk hing down uncanny nicksticks,
That aften gie the maidens sic licks,
As make them blyth to screen their faces
Wi hats and muckle maun *bon-graces*,
And cheat the lads that fain wad see
The glances o' a pauky ee,
Or gie their loves a wylie wink,
That erst might lend their hearts a clink.
Speak, was I made to dree the ladin
Of Gallic chairmen[4] heavy treadin,
Wha in my tender bouk bore holes
Wi waefu tackets i' the soals
O' broags, whilk on my body tramp,
And wound like death at ilka clamp?

CAUSEY
Weel crackit, friend – it aft hads true,
Wi naething fock make maist ado:

---

4 **Gallic chairmen**: Highland (Gaelic) sedan-chair carriers. Like the City Guard, Highlanders made up a large proportion of professions such as chairmen, porters etc.

Weel ken ye, tho' ye doughtna tell,
I pay the sairest kane[5] mysel;
Owr me ilk day big waggons rumble,
And a' my fabric birze and jumble;
Owr me the muckle horses gallop,
Enough to rug my very saul up;
And coachmen never trou they're sinning,
While down the street their wheels are spinning.
Like thee, do I not bide the brunt
Of Highland chairman's heavy dunt?
Yet I hae never thought o' breathing
Complaint, or making din for naething.

PLAINSTANES
Had sae, and lat me get a word in,
Your back's best fitted for the burden;
And I can eithly tell you why,
Ye're doughtier by far than I;
For whin-stanes, howkit frae the craigs,
May thole the prancing feet of naigs,
Nor ever fear uncanny hotches
Frae clumsy carts or hackney-coaches,
While I, a weak and feckless creature,
Am moulded by a safter nature.
Wi mason's chissel dighted neat,
To gar me look baith clean and feat,
I scarce can bear a sairer thump
Than comes frae sole of shoe or pump.
I grant, indeed, that, now and than,
Yield to a *paten's* pith I maun;
But patens,[6] tho' they're aften plenty,

---

[5] **kane**: rent paid to a landlord in kind, such as poultry, eggs, cheese; hence, any imposition.

[6] **patens**: wooden-soled shoes mounted on iron rings to raise the feet above the mud. "The *patten* saved the lower orders from the mud. The Old Assembly Close, where the original Assembly had a dancing-room (before my time), was among the first of the closes well paved, and therefore the greatest thoroughfare from the High

Are ay laid down wi feet fou tenty,
And stroaks frae ladies, tho' they're teazing,
I freely maun avow are pleasing.
　For what use was I made, I wonder,
It was na tamely to chap under
The weight of ilka codroch chiel
That does my skin to targets peel;
But gin I guess aright, my trade is
To fend frae skaith the bonny ladies,
To keep the bairnies free frae harms
Whan airing in their nurses' arms,
To be a safe and canny bield
For growing youth or drooping eild.
　Take then frae me the heavy load
Of burden-bearers heavy-shod,
Or, by my troth, the gude auld town shall
Hae this affair before their council.

CAUSEY
I dinna care a single jot,
Tho' summon'd by a shelly-coat,[7]
Sae leally I'll propone defences,
As get ye flung for my expenses;
Your libel I'll impugn *verbatim*,

　Street to the Cowgate. It was astonishing how the servant girls would run down it, steep as it was, with their high pattens on. I overheard one day a girl saying to her companion as they ran down that close, 'Jenny, do you not like to gar (make) your pattens clatter?'" (*The Anecdotes and Egotisms of Henry Mackenzie 1745–1831*, H.W. Thompson (ed.), Oxford, 1927, pp.46–7)

7 **shelly-coat**: here, a sheriff officer. But it also means a water-sprite covered in shells. Allan Ramsay, in a note to *The Gentle Shepherd*, Act I, scene i, l.78, explains: "One of these frightful Spectres the ignorant People are terrified at, and tell us strange Stories of; that they are clothed with a Coat of Shells, which make a horrid rattling, that they'll be sure to destroy one, if he gets not a running Water between him and it; it dares not meddle with a Woman with Child, &c."

And hae a *magnum damnum datum*;[8]
For tho' frae *Arthur's Seat* I sprang,
And am in constitution strang,
Wad it no fret the hardest stane
Beneath the *Luckenbooths*[9] to grane?
Tho' magistrates the *Cross* discard,
It makes na whan they leave the *Guard*,[10]
A lumbersome and stinkin bigging,
That rides the sairest on my rigging.
Poor me owr meikle do ye blame,
For tradesmen tramping on your wame,
Yet a' your advocates and braw fock
Come still to me 'twixt ane and twa 'clock,
And never yet were kend to range
At *Charlie's Statue* or *Exchange*.[11]
Then tak your beaux and macaronies,
Gie me trades-fock and country Johnies;
The deil's in't gin ye dinna sign
Your sentiments conjunct wi mine.

---

8 **magnum damnum datum:** if taken to court, Causey will defend himself so comprehensively as to win the case and recover all expenses, while the unsuccessful pursuer Plainstanes will incur a fine.
9 **Luckenbooths:** see note to 'Auld Reikie'.
10 **Cross and Guard:** i.e. though magistrates do away with the Cross, it makes no odds if they leave the guardhouse in place. The Mercat Cross was demolished in 1756 when the Royal Exchange (now the City Chambers) was built, but the guardhouse, a much bulkier construction right in the middle of the street, remained until 1785. The removal of the Cross was unpopular with many, whose disapproval was articulated by the lame poet James Wilson (d.1789), originally from Cumbernauld. Wilson, who styled himself 'Claudero', eked out a living running a school in the Cowgate and penned verses attacking the modernisers' enthusiasm for destroying medieval Edinburgh. He wrote a satirical poem entitled 'The Last Speech and Dying Words of the Cross of Edinburgh, which was hanged, drawn, and quartered, on Monday the 15th of March 1756, for the horrid crime of being an Incumbrance to the Street'.
11 **Charlie's Statue or Exchange:** lawyers and merchants habitually gathered to do business in the street, in spite of the spaces available to them in Parliament Square, where the equestrian statue of Charles II still stands, and the new Exchange across the street.

The City Guardhouse,
which stood in the High Street till 1785

PLAINSTANES
Gin we twa could be as auld-farrant
As gar the council gie a warrant,
Ilk loun rebellious to tak,
Wha walks not in the proper track,
And o' three shilling Scottish souk him,
Or in the *water-hole*[12] sair douk him;
This might assist the poor's collection,
And gie baith parties satisfaction.

CAUSEY
But first, I think it will be good
To bring it to the *Robinhood*,[13]
Whare we shall hae the question stated,
And keen and crabbitly debated,
Whether the provost and the bailies,
For the town's good whase daily toil is,
Should listen to our joint petitions,
And see obtemper'd the conditions.

---

12 **the water-hole**: possibly the reservoir on Castlehill.
13 **the Robinhood**: a newly constituted debating society, of which Fergusson was a member, which met weekly at the Thistle Lodge, Carrubber's Close. Drama, literature and public affairs were among the topics discussed.

PLAINSTANES
Content am I – but east the gate is
The sun, wha taks his leave of Thetis,[14]
And comes to wauken honest fock,
That gang to wark at sax o'clock;
It sets us to be dumb a while,
And let our words gie place to toil.

---

14 **Thetis:** see note to 'Hallow-Fair'.

The Rising of the Session

To a' men living be it kend,
The Session now is at an end:
Writers, your finger-nebbs unbend,
    And quat the pen,
Till Time wi lyart pow shall send
    Blyth June again.

Tired o' the law and a' its phrases,
The wylie *writers*,[1] rich as *Crœsus*,[2]
Hurl frae the town in hackney chaises,
    For country cheer:
The powny that in spring-time grazes,
    Thrives a' the year.

Ye lawyers, bid fareweel to lees,
Fareweel to din, fareweel to fees,
The canny hours o' rest may please
    Instead o' siller:
Hain'd multer hads the mill at ease,
    And finds the miller.[3]

Blyth they may be wha wanton play
In Fortune's bonny blinkin ray,

First published in *The Weekly Magazine*, 18 March 1773. The Court of Session, the highest civil court in Scotland, sat from mid-November to mid-March, and from mid-June to mid-August, with a three-week adjournment over Christmas and New Year.

1 **writers**: lawyers or law-agents; more loosely, all clerks.
2 **rich as Croesus**: Croesus, king of Lydia (560–546 BC), whose name has become proverbial for wealth.
3 **Hain'd multer**: multer was an amount of grain paid to a miller in return for grinding corn. Thus: "saved multer goes to the miller's store, and allows him to rest the mill."

Fu weel can they ding dool away
            Wi comrades couthy,
And never dree a hungert day,
            Or e'ening drouthy.

Ohon the day for him that's laid
In dowie poortith's caldrife shade,
Ablins owr honest for his trade,
            He racks his wits,
How he may get his bouk weel clad,
            And fill his guts.

The farmer's sons, as yap as sparrows,
Are glad, I trou, to flee the barras,
And whistle to the plough and harrows
            At barley seed:[4]
What writer wadna gang as far as
            He could for breid?

After their yokin, I wat weel
They'll stoo the kebbuck to the heel;
Eith can the plough-stilts gar a chiel
            Be unco vogie,
Clean to lick aff his crowdy-meal,
            And scart his cogie.

Now mony a fallow's dung adrift
To a' the blasts beneath the lift,
And tho' their stamack's aft in tift
            In vacance time,
Yet seenil do they ken the rift
            O' stappit weym.

---

4 **barley seed**: barley-sowing time.

Now gin a *notar* should be wanted,
You'll find the *pillars*[5] gayly planted;
For little thing *protests*[6] are granted
    Upo' a bill,
And weightiest matters covenanted
    For haf a gill.

Nae body taks a morning dribb
O' *Holland gin* frae *Robin Gibb*;[7]
And tho' a dram to Rob's mair sib
    Than is his wife,
He maun take time to daut his *Rib*
    Till siller's rife.

This vacance is a heavy doom
On *Indian Peter's* coffee-room,[8]

---

5 **pillars**: the pillars were, according to a note in the Chambers (1840) edition of Fergusson's *Poetical Works*, "an arcade skirting the passage leading into the Parliament Close – a great haunt of low writers [notars] as intimated in the text".

6 **protest**: a formal declaration, usually drawn up on request by a notary public, giving notice that, payment of a promissory note or bill of exchange having been refused, the holder intends to recover all expenses incurred as a result.

7 **Robin Gibb**: keeper of a tavern in the Outer House, the old Parliament Hall, which was then partly occupied by a number of small shops.

8 **Indian Peter's coffee-room**: Peter Williamson (1730–99) was one of the great characters of the town. As a boy of eight he had been kidnapped from the harbour at Aberdeen, taken to America and sold to a pioneer, a Perthshire man who raised him on the frontier. Freed at 17, Williamson married soon after, but was then captured by Indians and his home destroyed. After some months during which he was tortured and witnessed numerous atrocities, he escaped and returned to his father-in-law. He volunteered to fight the Indians, was then taken prisoner by the French, and after further mistreatment in captivity was sent to Plymouth via Quebec. He published a bestselling account of his adventures in 1758, but on returning to Aberdeen found himself being sued for libel, his book having implicated certain important local persons in his original kidnap. His book was burnt at the mercat cross by the hangman and he was fined and banished from the city. He settled in Edinburgh, where he opened his tavern in Old Parliament Close, calling him-

For a' his china pigs are toom;
    Nor do we see
In wine the sucker biskets soum
    As light's a flee.

But stop, my Muse, nor make a mane,
Pate disna fend on that alane;
He can fell twa dogs wi ae bane,
    While ither fock
Maun rest themsels content wi ane,
    Nor farrer trock.

Ye change-house keepers never grumble,
Tho' you a while your bickers whumble;
Be unco patientfu and humble,
    Nor make a din,
Tho' gude joot binna kend to rumble
    Your weym within.

You needna grudge to draw your breath
For little mair than haf a reath,[9]
Than, gin we a' be spar'd frae death,
    We'll gladly prie
Fresh noggans o' your reaming graith
    Wi blythsome glee.

---

self "Peter Williamson from the Other World". He refought his libel case against his enemies in Aberdeen and won. As Fergusson indicates, his tavern was not his only business. He ventured into printing and bookselling, and produced the first Edinburgh street directory and its first penny postal service. The latter was taken over by the Government in 1791, in return for which he received compensation of £25 per annum for life.

9 **haf a reath**: a reath or raith is a period of three months, a quarter-term. The middle six or eight weeks between sessions would presumably be the quietest for the tavern-keepers.

Ode to the Bee

Herds, blythsome tune your canty reeds,
And welcome to the gowany meads
The pride o' a' the insect thrang,
A stranger to the green sae lang;
Unfald ilk buss and ilka brier,
The bounties o' the gleesome year,
To him whase voice delights the spring,
Whase soughs the saftest slumbers bring.

The trees in simmer-cleething drest,
The hillocks in their greenest vest,
The brawest flow'rs rejoic'd we see,
Disclose their sweets, and ca' on thee,
Blythly to skim on wanton wing
Thro' a' the fairy haunts of spring.

Whan fields hae got their dewy gift,
And dawnin breaks upo' the lift,
Then gang your wa's thro' hight and howe,
Seek caller haugh or sunny knowe,
Or ivy'd craig, or burnbank brae,
Whare industry shall bid ye gae,
For hiney or for waxen store,
To ding sad poortith frae your door.

Could feckless creature, man, be wise,
The simmer o' his life to prize,
In winter he might fend fu bauld,

First published in *The Weekly Magazine*, 29 April 1773. Broomhouse, an estate in the parish of Spott, just south of Dunbar, was not far from North Belton, the estate of James Hay, which Fergusson visited on several occasions (and for the whole of August 1773) with his friend Charles Lorimer.

His eild unkend to nippin cauld,
Yet thir, alas! are antrin fock
That lade their scape[1] wi winter stock.
Auld age maist feckly glowrs right dour
Upo' the ailings of the poor,
Wha hope for nae comforting, save
That dowie dismal house, the grave.
Then, feeble man, be wise, take tent
How industry can fetch content:
Behad the bees whare'er they wing,
Or thro' the bonny bow'rs of spring,
Whare vi'lets or whare roses blaw,
And siller dew-draps nightly fa,
Or whan on open bent they're seen,
On heather-bell or thristle green;
The hiney's still as sweet that flows
Frae thistle cald or kendling rose.

    Frae this the human race may learn
Reflection's hiney'd draps to earn,
Whether they tramp life's thorny way,
Or thro' the sunny vineyard stray.

    Instructive bee! attend me still,
Owr a' my labours sey your skill:
For thee shall hiney-suckles rise,
With lading to your busy thighs,
And ilka shrub surround my cell,
Whareon ye like to hum and dwell:
My trees in bourachs owr my ground
Shall fend ye frae ilk blast o' wind;
Nor e'er shall herd, wi ruthless spike,
Delve out the treasures frae your byke,
But in my fence be safe, and free
To live, and work, and sing like me.

---

1 **scape**: skep, bee-hive.

Like thee, by fancy wing'd, the Muse
Scuds ear' and heartsome owr the dews,
Fu vogie, and fu blyth to crap
The winsome flow'rs frae Nature's lap,
Twining her living garlands there,
That lyart time can ne'er impair.

*Broomhouse, East-Lothian,
April 26, 1773.*

The Farmer's Ingle

> Et multo in primis hilarans convivia Baccho,
> Ante focum, si frigus erit.
> —*Virgil, Eclogue V*

Whan gloaming grey out owr the welkin keeks,
    Whan Batie ca's his owsen to the byre,
Whan Thrasher John, sair dung, his barn-door steeks,
    And lusty lasses at the dighting tire:
What bangs fu leal the e'enings coming cauld,
    And gars snaw-tappit winter freeze in vain;
Gars dowie mortals look baith blyth and bauld,
    Nor fley'd wi a' the poortith o' the plain –
Begin, my Muse, and chant in hamely strain.

Frae the big stack, weel winnow't on the hill,
    Wi divets theekit frae the weet and drift,
Sods, peats, and heath'ry trufs the chimley fill,
    And gar their thick'ning smeek salute the lift;
The gudeman, new come hame, is blyth to find,
    Whan he out owr the halland flings his een,
That ilka turn is handled to his mind,
    That a' his housie looks sae cosh and clean;
For cleanly house loos he, tho' e'er sae mean.

Weel kens the gudewife that the pleughs[1] require
    A heartsome meltith, and refreshing synd
O' nappy liquor, owr a bleezing fire:

First published in *The Weekly Magazine*, 13 May 1773; reprinted in *The Perth Magazine of Knowledge and Pleasure*, 21 May 1773. The quotation from Virgil translates: 'Cheering the feast with much wine in front of the fire, when winter comes.' The debt owed to this poem by Burns's 'The Cotter's Saturday Night' is obvious.

1 **pleughs**: ploughmen.

Sair wark and poortith downa weel be join'd.
Wi butter'd bannocks now the girdle reiks,
  I' the far nook the bowie briskly reams;
The readied kail stand by the chimley cheeks,
  And had the riggin het wi welcome steams,
  Whilk than the daintiest kitchen nicer seems.

Frae this lat gentler gabs a lesson lear;
  Wad they to labouring lend an eident hand,
They'd rax fell strang upo' the simplest fare,
  Nor find their stamacks ever at a stand.
Fu hale and healthy wad they pass the day,
  At night in calmest slumbers dose fu sound,
Nor doctor need their weary life to spae,
  Nor drogs their noddle and their sense confound,
  Till death slip sleely on, and gie the hindmost wound.

On siccan food has mony a doughty deed
  By Caledonia's ancestors been done;
By this did mony wight fu weirlike bleed
  In brulzies frae the dawn to set o' sun:
'Twas this that brac'd their gardies, stiff and strang,
  That bent the deidly yew in ancient days,
Laid Denmark's daring sons on yird alang,[2]
  Gar'd Scottish thristles bang the Roman bays;[3]
  For near our crest their heads they doughtna raise.

---

[2] **Laid Denmark's daring sons on yird alang**: probably a reference to the battle at Luncarty, Perthshire, in which Kenneth III (d.1005) is supposed to have defeated the Danes. This victory was achieved after the founder of the Hay family, who had been working his fields near the confrontation of the two armies, prevented the Scots from fleeing by blocking their retreat in a narrow pass and knocking them down with his plough yoke till they turned and faced the enemy again. The fact that Fergusson was spending much time at North Belton, the estate of James Hay, may have brought this story to mind.

[3] **thristles** and **bays**: respective national emblems of the Scots and Romans. To be crowned with bays was the customary Roman way of acknowledging a victorious general.

The couthy cracks begin whan supper's owr,
   The cheering bicker gars them glibly gash
O' simmer's showery blinks and winters sour,
   Whase floods did erst their mailins' produce hash:
'Bout kirk and market eke their tales gae on,
   How Jock woo'd Jenny here to be his bride,
And there how Marion, for a bastard son,
   Upo' the cutty-stool was forc'd to ride,
   The waefu scald o' our Mess John[4] to bide.

The fient a cheep's amang the bairnies noo;
   For a' their anger's wi their hunger gane:
Ay maun the childer, wi a fastin mou,
   Grumble and greet, and make an unco mane,
In rangles round before the ingle's lowe:
   Frae gudame's[5] mouth auld warld tale they hear,
O' warlocks louping round the wirrikow,
   O' ghaists that win in glen and kirk-yard drear,
   Whilk touzles a' their tap, and gars them shak wi fear.

For weel she trous that fiends and fairies be
   Sent frae the deil to fleetch us to our ill;
That kye hae tint their milk wi evil ee,
   And corn been scowder'd on the glowing kill.[6]
O mock na this, my friends! but rather mourn,
   Ye in life's brawest spring wi reason clear,
Wi eild our idle fancies a' return,
   And dim our dolefu days wi bairnly fear;
   The mind's ay cradled whan the grave is near.

Yet thrift, industrious, bides her latest days,
   Tho' age her sair dow'd front wi runcles wave,

---

4 **Mess John**: common (often jocular) term for a kirk minister.
5 **gudame**: granny.
6 **kill**: kiln.

Yet frae the russet lap the spindle plays,
   Her e'enin stent reels she as weel's the lave.
On some feast-day, the wee-things buskit braw
   Shall heeze her heart up wi a silent joy,
Fu cadgie that her head was up and saw
   Her ain spun cleething on a darling oy,
   Careless tho' death should make the feast her foy.

In its auld lerroch yet the deas remains,
   Whare the gudeman aft streeks him at his ease,
A warm and canny lean for weary banes
   O' lab'rers doil'd upo' the wintry leas:
Round him will baudrins and the colly come,
   To wag their tail, and cast a thankfu ee
To him wha kindly flings them mony a crumb
   O' kebbuck whang'd, and dainty fadge to prie;
   This a' the boon they crave, and a' the fee.

Frae him the lads their morning counsel tak,
   What stacks he wants to thrash, what rigs to till;
How big a birn maun lie on bassie's back,
   For meal and multer to the thirling mill.[7]
Neist the gudewife her hireling damsels bids
   Glowr thro' the byre, and see the hawkies bound,
Take tent case Crummy tak her wonted tids,[8]
   And ca the laiglen's treasure on the ground,
   Whilk spills a kebbuck nice, or yellow pound.

Then a' the house for sleep begin to grien,
   Their joints to slack frae industry a while;

---

7 **multer to the thirling mill**: the thirling mill was the mill to which a bound (thirled) tenant had to take his grain for grinding. See note to 'The Rising of the Session'.
8 **Take tent case Crummy tak her wonted tids**: beware lest Crummy [pet name for a cow, especially one with crooked horns] be in one of her usual bad moods.

The leaden god fa's heavy on their een,
  And haflins steeks them frae their daily toil:
The cruizy too can only blink and bleer,
  The restit ingle's done the maist it dow;
Tacksman and cottar⁹ eke to bed maun steer,
  Upo' the cod to clear the drumly pow,
  Till wauken'd by the dawning's ruddy glow.

Peace to the husbandman and a' his tribe,
  Whase care fells a' our wants frae year to year;
Lang may his sock and couter turn the gleyb,
  And bauks o' corn bend down wi laded ear.¹⁰
May Scotia's simmers ay look gay and green,
  Her yellow har'sts frae scowry blasts decreed;
May a' her tenants sit fu snug and bien,
  Frae the hard grip of ails and poortith freed,
  And a lang lasting train o' peaceful hours succeed.

---

9 **Tacksman and cottar:** the holder of a tack or tenancy of a farm, and the farmworker whose cottage is provided in return for his labour.
10 **And bauks o' corn bend down wi laded ear:** i.e. and may rigs as yet unploughed bear corn bent with grain-loaded ears.

The Ghaists: A Kirk-yard Eclogue

> Did you not say, in good Ann's day,
>   And vow and did protest, Sir,
> That when Hanover should come o'er,
>   We surely should be blest, Sir?
> > — *An auld Sang made new again*

Whare the braid planes[1] in dowie murmurs wave
Their ancient taps out owr the cald, clad grave,
Whare Geordie Girdwood,[2] mony a lang-spun day,
Houkit for gentlest banes the humblest clay,
Twa sheeted ghaists, sae grizly and sae wan,
'Mang lanely tombs their dowf discourse began.

First published in *The Weekly Magazine*, 27 May 1773. The two characters of this poem are George Watson (1654–1723), merchant and banker, and George Heriot (1563–1624), goldsmith and financier to James VI. Both men were wealthy philanthropists who endowed charitable schools or "hospitals" in Edinburgh for the education of the sons of poor or deceased Edinburgh burgesses. (The schools are now fee-paying independents.) The endowments were held in trust and administered by boards of governors. In 1773, in an effort to raise the value of its own securities, the Government proposed the Mortmain Bill, which would empower the trustees of such charities to invest all their available moneys in a government fund, at a rate of three per cent. An annuity would be paid back annually to cover the charities' costs. Objections were raised that this would discourage future benefactors from leaving large sums for charitable purposes if they could not predetermine how those sums should be administered; and in particular many Scots disliked the idea of endowments for specifically Scottish purposes being syphoned off to service the national debt in London, especially at a fixed and low rate of interest. Town councils, including Edinburgh and Glasgow, petitioned against the Mortmain Bill, and in the end it did not become law.

1 **planes**: plane-trees.
2 **Geordie Girdwood**: the former sexton of Greyfriars Kirkyard, which lies just east of George Heriot's School. Watson's Hospital faced Heriot's from the south, across what is now Lauriston Place.

WATSON

Cauld blaws the nippin north wi angry sough,
And showers his hailstanes frae the Castle Cleugh
Owr the Greyfriars, whare, at mirkest hour,
Bogles and spectres wont to tak their tour,
Harlin the pows and shanks to hidden cairns,
Amang the hamlocks wild and sun-burnt fearns;
But nane the night save you and I hae come
Frae the dern mansions of the midnight tomb.
Now whan the dawning's near, whan cock maun craw,
And wi his angry bougil gar's withdraw,
Ayont the kirk we'll stap, and there tak bield,
While the black hours our nightly freedom yield.

HERRIOT

I'm weel content; but binna cassen doun,
Nor trou the cock will ca ye hame owr soon,
For tho' the eastern lift betakens day,
Changing her rokelay black for mantle grey,
Nae weirlike bird our knell of parting rings,
Nor sheds the caller moisture frae his wings.
Nature has chang'd her course; the birds o' day
Dosen in silence on the bending spray,
While owlets round the craigs at noon-tide flee,
And bludey bawks sit singand[3] on the tree.
Ah, Caledon! the land I yence held dear,
Sair mane mak I for thy destruction near;
And thou, Edina! anes my dear abode,
Whan royal Jamie sway'd the sovereign rod,
In thae blest days, weel did I think bestow'd,
To blaw thy poortith by wi heaps o' gowd;
To mak thee sonsy seem wi mony a gift,
And gar thy stately turrets speel the lift:

---

3 **singand**: an archaic form, which Fergusson occasionally uses for the present participle.

In vain did Danish Jones,⁴ wi gimcrack pains,
In Gothic sculpture fret the pliant stanes:
In vain did he affix my statue here,
Brawly to busk wi flow'rs ilk coming year;⁵
My tow'rs are sunk, my lands are barren now,
My fame, my honour, like my flow'rs, maun dow.

WATSON
Sure Major Weir,⁶ or some sic warlock wight,
Has flung beguilin glamer owr your sight;
Or else some kittle cantrup thrown, I ween,
Has bound in mirlygoes my ain twa een,
If ever aught frae sense could be believ'd
(And seenil hae my senses been deceiv'd),
This moment, owr the tap of Adam's tomb,⁷
Fu easy can I see your chiefest dome:
Nae corbie fleein there, nor croupin craws,
Seem to forspeak the ruin of thy haws,
But a' your tow'rs in wonted order stand,
Steeve as the rocks that hem our native land.

HERRIOT
Think na I vent my well-a-day in vain;
Kent ye the cause, ye sure wad join my mane.

---

4 **Danish Jones**: Inigo Jones, who for long was erroneously believed to have been the architect of Heriot's Hospital. Fergusson calls him "Danish" because he worked for a period at the Danish court, designing the palace of Frederiksborg. In fact, Heriot's was begun by William Wallace and William Ayton, and completed by John and Robert Mylne, Master Masons of Scotland, around 1693.
5 **to busk wi flow'rs**: on the first Monday of June every year, pupils pay tribute to Heriot's benevolence in the Buskin ceremony, when his statue is garlanded with flowers.
6 **Major Weir**: Thomas Weir (c.1600–1670), the "wizard of the West Bow", was a seemingly devout Presbyterian discovered to have committed crimes of incest and bestiality, and widely believed, with his sister Jean, to have practised witchcraft. Both were executed in 1670.
7 **Adam's tomb**: the grandiose burial place of William Adam (1689–1748), architect and father of Robert and James Adam.

Black be the day that e'er to England's ground
Scotland was eikit by the Union's bond;
For mony a menzie of destructive ills
The country now maun brook frae *mortmain bills*,
That void our test'ments, and can freely gie
Sic will and scoup to the ordain'd trustee,
That he may tirr our stateliest riggins bare,
Nor acres, houses, woods, nor fishins spare,
Till he can lend the stoitering state a lift
Wi gowd in gowpins as a grassum gift;[8]
In lieu o' whilk, we maun be weel content
To tyne the capital at *three per cent*.
A doughty sum indeed, whan now-a-days
They raise provisions as the stents they raise,[9]
Yoke hard the poor, and lat the rich chiels be,
Pamper'd at ease wi ithers' industry.
   Hale interest for my fund can scantly noo
Cleed a' my callants' backs, and stap their mou:
How maun their weyms wi sairest hunger slack,
Their duds in targets flaff upo' their back,
Whan they are doom'd to keep a lasting Lent,
Starving for England's weel at *three per cent*.

WATSON
Auld Reikie than may bless the gowden times,
Whan honesty and poortith baith are crimes:
She little kend, whan you and I endow'd
Our hospitals for back-gaun burghers gude,
That e'er our siller or our lands should bring
A gude bien living to a back-gaun king,

---

8 **grassum gift**: grassum was the sum paid by a tenant to his landlord on the granting or renewal of a lease. Fergusson is implying that the effect of the Mortmain Bill will be to put trustees into a tenant-landlord relationship with the state.
9 **They raise provisions as the stents they raise**: i.e. the cost of goods rises at the same rate as property taxes.

Wha, thanks to ministry! is grown sae wise,
He downa chew the bitter cud of vice;
For gin, frae Castlehill to Netherbow,
Wad honest houses bawdy-houses grow,
The Crown wad never spier the price o' sin,
Nor hinder younkers to the deil to rin;
But gif some mortal grien for pious fame,
And leave the poor man's pray'r to sain his name,
His gear maun a' be scatter'd by the claws
O' ruthless, ravenous, and harpy laws.
Yet, should I think, altho' the bill tak place,
The council winna lack sae meikle grace
As lat our heritage at wanworth gang,
Or the succeeding generations wrang
O' braw bien maintenance and walth o' lear,
Whilk else had drappit to their children's skair;
For mony a deep and mony a rare ingyne
Hae sprung frae Herriot's wark, and sprung frae mine.

HERRIOT
I find, my friend, that ye but little ken,
There's eenow on the earth a set o' men,
Wha, if they get their private pouches lin'd,
Gie na a winnelstrae for a' mankind;
They'll sell their country, flae their conscience bare,
To gar the weigh-bauk turn a single hair.
The government need only bait the line
Wi the prevailing flee, the gowden coin,
Then our executors, and wise trustees,
Will sell them fishes in forbidden seas,
Upo' their dwyning country girn in sport,
Laugh in their sleeve, and get a place at court.

WATSON
Ere that day come, I'll 'mang our spirits pick
Some ghaist that trokes and conjures wi Auld Nick,
To gar the wind wi rougher rumbles blaw,

And weightier thuds than ever mortal saw:
Fire-flaught and hail, wi ten-fald fury's fires,
Shall lay yird-laigh Edina's airy spires;
Tweed shall rin rowtin down his banks out owr,
Till Scotland's out o' reach o' England's pow'r;
Upo' the briny Borean jaws to float,
And mourn in dowy soughs her dowy lot.

HERRIOT
Yonder's the tomb of wise Mackenzie[10] fam'd,
Whase laws rebellious bigotry reclaim'd,
Freed the hale land o' covenanting fools,
Wha erst hae fash'd us wi unnumber'd dools;
Till night we'll tak the swaird aboon our pows,
And than, whan she her ebon chariot rowes,
We'll travel to the vaut wi stealing stap,
And wauk Mackenzie frae his quiet nap:
Tell him our ails, that he, wi wonted skill,
May fleg the schemers o' the *mortmain bill*.

---

10 **wise Mackenzie**: Sir George Mackenzie of Rosehaugh (1636–91), known by the Covenanters as the Bluidy Mackenzie for his active prosecution of them as King's Advocate. Fergusson seems rather to have admired him as a suppressor of "rebellious bigotry", as an opponent of union with England, and as the founder of the Advocates' Library, later the National Library of Scotland. Mackenzie's gloomy mausoleum is on the south wall of Greyfriars, and by tradition boys would test their courage and his fearsome reputation by approaching at nightfall and calling, "Bluidy Mackenzie, come oot if ye daur! Lift the sneck and draw the baur!"

Epistles Between Andrew Gray and Robert Fergusson

TO R. FERGUSSON

Deed[1] R. I e'en man dip my pen,
But how to write I dinna ken;
For learning, I got fint a grain,
    To tell me how
To write to ony gentleman,
      Sic like as you.

How blyth am I whan I do see
A piece o' your fine poetrie,
It gars me laugh fou merrilie,
    Because there's nane
That gies sic great insight to me,
      As yours itlane.

Trouth, Fergusson, I'm verry shier,
(Therefore I think I need na spier)
That ye dwalt anes abien the mier.[2]
    For ye do crack
The very sam way we do here
      At Amond back.

First published in *The Perth Magazine of Knowledge and Pleasure*, 11 June 1773. The author was possibly Dr Andrew Gray, minister at Abernethy in Perthshire, on the south side of the Tay, and a well-known humourist. As the internal evidence of the poem (invented or unidentified place-names, uncertain geography, and the deliberately overdone dialect which seems much more characteristic of the north-east than of Perthshire) is confusing, this identification is impossible to prove or disprove. For a discussion of this, see Matthew P. McDiarmid's note in *The Poems of Robert Fergusson* (Scottish Text Society, Vol.II, 1956), p.290.

1 **Deed**: indeed, in the sense of 'Upon my word!'
2 **abien the mier**: above the moor. Presumably Tippermuir, west of Perth, north of which flows the Almond.

Ye've English plain enough nae doubt,
And Latin too, but ye do suit
Your lines, to fock that's out about
    'Mang hills and braes:
This is the thing that gars me shout
    Sae loud your praise.

Gin ever ye come here awa,
I hope ye'll be sae gude as ca,
For Andrew Gray, at Whistle-ha,
    The riddle macker,[3]
About a riglength frae Coolsa,
    Just o'er the water.

We's treat ye, lad, for doing sae weel,
Wi bannocks o' guid barley meal,
And wi as mony cabbage kail
    As ye can tak:
And twa three chappins o' guid ale,
    To gar ye crack.

Whan this ye see, tak up your pen
And write word back to me again:
And fou you are,[4] mind lat me ken
    Without delay;
To hear ye're weel, I'll be right fain;
    Yours, Andrew Gray.

Whistle-ha', June 1st, 1773.

---

3 **The riddle macker:** a pun, meaning maker of both sieves and puzzles, which tends to support the authorship of Dr Gray.
4 **fou you are:** how you are.

To Andrew Gray

Nae langer bygane, than the streen,
Your couthy letter met my een;
I lang to wag a cutty speen
      On Amond water;
And claw the lips o' truncher treen
      And tak a clatter.

"Frae *Whistleha*" your muse doth cry;
Whare'er ye win I carena by;
Ye're no the laird o' *Whistledry*,
      As lang's ye can
Wi routh o' reikin kail supply
      The inward man.

You'll trou me, Billy, kail's fu geed
To synd an' peerify the bleid;
'Twill rin like ony scarlet reid,
      While patt ye put on,
Wi wethers that round Amond feed,
      The primest mutton.

Ane wad maist think ye'd been at Scoon,
Whan kings wure there the Scottish croun;
A soupler or mair fleetching loun
      Ne'er hap'd on hurdies,
Whan courtiers' tongues war there in tune,
      For oily wordies.

Can you nae ither theme divine
To blaw upon, but *my* ingyne?

First published in *The Perth Magazine of Knowledge and Pleasure*, 2 July 1773. Fergusson adopts the same dialect as his correspondent.

At *nature* keek, she's unco fine
    Redd up, and braw;
And can gie scouth to *muses nine*
    At *Whistle-ha*.

Her road awhile is rough an' round,
An' few poetic gowans found;
The stey braes o' the muses' ground
    We scarce can crawl up;
But on the tap we're light as wind
    To scour an' gallop.

Whan first ye seyd to mak a riddle
Ye'd hae an unco fike an' piddle,
An' ablins brak aff i' the middle,
    Like Samy Butler:[1]
'Tis e'en sae wi Apollo's fiddle,
    Before we wit lear.

Then flegna at this weary practice,
That's taen to get this wyly nack nice;
The eident muse begins to crack wise,
    An' ne'er cry dule:
It's *idleseat*, that banefu black vice,
    That gars her cool.

Andrew, at *Whistleha*, your een
May lippen for me very sien:
For barley scones my grinders grien.
    They're special eating;
Wi bizzin cogs that ream abien,
    Our thrapple weeting.

---

[1] **Samy Butler**: Samuel Butler (1612–80), the English author of *Hudibras*, a mock-heroic poem which satirises the hypocrisy of Presbyterians and Independents. In form based on *Don Quixote*, it charts the adventures of a grotesque Puritan and his squire Ralpho, and is marked by Rabelaisian humour and complex rhymes.

Till than may you had hale and fier,
That we to *maltman's browst* may steer,
And ilka care and ilka fear
      To dogdrive ding;[2]
While cheek for chow we laugh and jeer,
      And crack and sing.

R. Fergusson.
Edinburgh, June 23, 1773.

---

2 **ilka care and ilka fear to dogdrive ding:** i.e. send every care and fear to the dogs.

On Seeing a Butterfly in the Street

Daft gowk, in macaroni dress,
Are ye come here to shew your face,
Bowden wi pride o' simmer gloss,
To cast a dash at Reikie's cross;
And glowr at mony twa-legg'd creature,
Flees braw by art, tho' worms by nature?

  Like country laird in city cleeding,
Ye're come to town to lear good breeding;
To bring ilk darling toast and fashion
In vogue amang the flee creation,
That they, like buskit belles and beaus,
May crook their mou fu sour at those
Whase weird is still to creep, alas!
Unnotic'd 'mang the humble grass;
While you, wi wings new buskit trim,
Can far frae yird and reptiles skim;
Newfangle grown wi new-got form,
You soar aboon your mither worm.

  Kind Nature lent but for a day
Her wings to make ye sprush and gay;
In her habuliments a while
Ye may your former sel beguile,
And ding awa the vexing thought
Of hourly dwyning into nought,
By beenging to your foppish brithers,
Black corbies dress'd in peacocks' feathers;
Like thee, they dander here an' there,

First published in *The Weekly Magazine*, 24 June 1773.

Whan simmer's blinks are warm an' fair,
An' loo to snuff the healthy balm
Whan ev'nin' spreads her wing sae calm;
But whan she girns an' glowrs sae dour
Frae Borean houff in angry show'r,
Like thee they scoug frae street or field,
An' hap them in a lyther bield;
For they war never made to dree
The adverse gloom o' Fortune's ee,
Nor ever pried life's pining woes,
Nor pu'd the prickles wi the rose.

   Poor butterfly! thy case I mourn;
To green kail-yeard and fruits return:
How could you troke the mavis' note
For *"penny pies all piping hot"*?
Can lintie's music be compar'd
Wi gruntles frae the City Guard?
Or can our flow'rs at ten-hours' bell
The gowan or the spink excel?

   Now should our sclates wi hailstanes ring,
What cabbage-fald wad screen your wing?
Say, fluttering fairy! wer't thy hap
To light beneath braw Nany's cap,
Wad she, proud butterfly of May!
In pity lat you skaithless stay?
The furies glancing frae her een
Wad rug your wings o' siller sheen,
That, wae for thee! far, far outvy
Her Paris artist's finest dye;
Then a' your bonny spraings wad fall,
An' you a worm be left to crawl.

   To sic mishanter rins the laird
Wha quats his ha-house an' kail-yeard,

Grows politician, scours to court,
Whare he's the laughing-stock and sport
Of Ministers, wha jeer an' jibe,
And heeze his hopes wi thought o' bribe,
Till in the end they flae him bare,
Leave him to poortith, and to care.
Their fleetching words owr late he sees,
He trudges hame, repines and dees.

   Sic be their fa wha dirk thereben
In blackest business no their ain;
And may they scad their lips fu leal,
That dip their spoons in ither's kail.

Auld Reikie, June 21. [1773]

Hame Content : A Satire

To all whom it may concern.

Some fock, like bees, fu glegly rin
To bykes bang'd fu o' strife and din,
And thieve and huddle crumb by crumb,
Till they have scrapt the dautit plumb,[1]
Then craw fell crously o' their wark,
Tell owr their turners mark by mark,
Yet darna think to lowse the pose,[2]
To aid their neighbours' ails and woes.

Gif gowd can fetter thus the heart,
And gar us act sae base a part,
Shall man, a niggard near-gawn elf!
Rin to the tether's end for pelf;
Learn ilka cunzied scoundrel's trick,
Whan a's done sell his saul to Nick?
I trou they've coft the purchase dear,
That gang sic lengths for warldly gear.

Now whan the dog-day heats[3] begin
To birsel and to peel the skin,
May I lie streekit at my ease,
Beneath the caller shady trees,
(Far frae the din o' Borrowstown)
Whare water plays the haughs bedown,

First published in *The Weekly Magazine*, 8 July 1773.
1 **plumb**: £100,000; loosely, a huge sum of money. So, "till they have taken a scraping off the darling pile".
2 **lowse the pose**: release the funds.
3 **dog-day heats**: the dog-days (the Romans called them *caniculares dies*) are the hottest days of the year, from early July to 11 August, when the dog-star Sirius rises with the sun, thus in theory adding to the overall temperature.

To jook the simmer's rigour there,
And breathe a while the caller air
'Mang herds, an' honest cottar fock,
That till the farm and feed the flock;
Careless o' mair, wha never fash
To lade their kist wi' useless cash,
But thank the gods for what they've sent
O' health eneugh, and blyth content,
An' pith, that helps them to stravaig
Owr ilka cleugh and ilka craig,
Unkend to a' the weary granes
That aft arise frae gentler banes,
On easy-chair that pamper'd lie,
Wi banefu viands gustit high,
And turn and fald their weary clay,
To rax and gaunt the live-lang day.

   Ye sages, tell, was man e'er made
To dree this hatefu sluggard trade?
Steekit frae Nature's beauties a'
That daily on his presence ca;
At hame to girn, and whinge, and pine
For fav'rite dishes, fav'rite wine:
Come then, shake off thir sluggish ties,
And wi the bird o' dawning rise;
On ilka bauk the clouds hae spread
Wi blobs o' dew a pearly bed;
Frae falds nae mair the owsen rout,
But to the fatt'ning claver lout,
Whare they may feed at heart's content,
Unyokit frae their winter's stent.

   Unyoke then, man, an' binna sweer
To ding a hole in ill-hain'd gear;[4]

---

4 **binna sweer to ding a hole in ill-hain'd gear**: do not shrink from making inroads into uselessly hoarded riches.

O think that eild, wi wyly fitt,
Is wearing nearer bit by bit;
Gin yence he claws you wi his paw,
What's siller for? Fiend haet awa,
But gowden playfair, that may please
The second sharger[5] till he dees.

Some daft chiel reads, and takes advice;
The chaise is yokit in a trice;
Awa drives he like huntit deil,
And scarce tholes time to cool his wheel,
Till he's Lord kens how far awa,
At Italy, or Well o' Spaw,[6]
Or to Montpelier's safter air;
For far aff fowls hae feathers fair.

There rest him weel; for eith can we
Spare mony glakit gowks like he;
They'll tell whare Tibur's waters rise;
What sea receives the drumly prize,
That never wi their feet hae mett
The marches o' their ain estate.

The Arno and the Tibur lang
Hae run fell clear in Roman sang;
But, save the reverence of schools!
They're baith but lifeless dowy pools.
Dought they compare wi bonny Tweed,
As clear as ony lammer-bead?
Or are their shores mair sweet and gay
Than Fortha's haughs or banks o' Tay?

---

5 **the second sharger**: a sharger is the runt of a litter. The sense here is, "What's the use of hoarding money till old age grips you? The only one to benefit is the runt who inherits it all."
6 **Well o' Spaw**: Spa, in Belgium.

Tho' there the herds can jink the show'rs
'Mang thriving vines an' myrtle bow'rs,
And blaw the reed to kittle strains,
While echo's tongue commends their pains,
Like ours, they canna warm the heart
Wi simple, saft, bewitching art.
On Leader haughs an' Yarrow braes,[7]
Arcadian herds wad tyne their lays,
To hear the mair melodious sounds
That live on our poetic grounds.

   Come, Fancy, come, and let us tread
The simmer's flow'ry velvet bed,
And a' your springs delighfu lowse
On Tweeda's banks or Cowdenknowes,[8]
That, taen wi thy inchanting sang,
Our Scottish lads may round ye thrang,
Sae pleas'd, they'll never fash again
To court you on Italian plain;
Soon will they guess ye only wear
The simple garb o' Nature here;
Mair comely far, an' fair to sight
Whan in her easy cleething dight,
Than in disguise ye was before
On Tibur's, or on Arno's shore.

   O Bangour![9] now the hills and dales
Nae mair gie back thy tender tales!

---

7 **On Leader haughs an' Yarrow braes:** a reference to the song 'Leader Haughs and Yarrow', published in Ramsay's *Tea-Table Miscellany* (1724).

8 **On Tweeda's banks or Cowdenknowes:** references to well-known songs: either 'Tweed-Side' or 'The Banks of Tweed', and 'The Broom of Cowdenknowes'. See note to 'Elegy, on the Death of Scots Music'.

9 **Bangour:** William Hamilton (1704–54) of Bangour, poet and author of 'The Braes of Yarrow'. See note to 'Elegy, on the Death of Scots Music'.

The birks on Yarrow now deplore
Thy mournfu muse has left the shore:
Near what bright burn or crystal spring
Did you your winsome whistle hing?
The muse shall there, wi wat'ry ee,
Gie the dunk swaird a tear for thee;
And Yarrow's genius, dowy dame!
Shall there forget her blude-stain'd stream,
On thy sad grave to seek repose,
Wha mourn'd her fate, condol'd her woes.

LEITH RACES

In July month, ae bonny morn,
   Whan Nature's rokelay green
Was spread owr ilka rigg o' corn
   To charm our roving een;
Glowring about I saw a quean,
   The fairest 'neath the lift;
Her een ware o' the siller sheen,
   Her skin like snawy drift,
                Sae white that day.

Quod she, "I ferly unco sair,
   That ye sud musand[1] gae,
Ye wha hae sung o' Hallow-fair,
   Her winter's pranks and play:
Whan on Leith-Sands the racers rare,
   Wi Jocky louns are met,
Their orra pennies there to ware,
   And drown themsels in debt
                Fu deep that day."

An' wha are ye, my winsome dear,
   That takes the gate sae early?
Whare do ye win, gin ane may spier?
   For I right meikle ferly,
That sic braw buskit laughing lass

   First published in *The Weekly Magazine*, 22 July 1773. The races were run 20–24 July. Burns's 'Holy Fair', with its rustic muse Fun, was heavily influenced by 'Leith Races' and Fergusson's slightly more other-worldly Mirth.

1 **musand**: an archaic form, perhaps derived from Allan Ramsay's use of it in his deliberately antique poem 'The Vision'.

    Thir bonny blinks should gie,
An' loup like Hebe[2] owr the grass,
    As wanton and as free
              Frae dule this day.

"I dwall amang the caller springs
    That weet the Land o' Cakes,
And aften tune my canty strings
    At bridals and late-wakes:[3]
They ca me Mirth; I ne'er was kend
    To grumble or look sour,
But blyth wad be a lift to lend,
    Gif ye wad sey my pow'r
              An' pith this day."

A bargain be't, and, by my fegs,
    Gif ye will be my mate,
Wi you I'll screw the cheery pegs,
    Ye shanna find me blate;
We'll reel an' ramble thro' the sands,
    And jeer wi a' we meet;
Nor hip the daft and gleesome bands
    That fill Edina's street
              Sae thrang this day.

Ere servant maids had wont to rise
    To seeth the breakfast kettle,
Ilk dame her brawest ribbon tries,
    To put her on her mettle,

---

2 **Hebe**: in Greek myth, the daughter of Zeus and Hera. The goddess of youth, she was able to restore men to their former youth and vigour.
3 **late-wakes**: it was an established custom that a wake could turn into a party, with music and dancing through the night; hence, Mirth's presence is not inappropriate.

Wi wiles some silly chiel to trap
   (And troth he's fain to get her),
But she'll craw kniefly in his crap,[4]
   Whan, wow! he canna flit her
               Frae hame that day.

Now, mony a scaw'd and bare-ars'd loun
   Rise early to their wark,
Enough to fley a muckle toun,
   Wi dinsome squeal and bark.
"Here is the true an' faithfu list
   O' noblemen and horses;
Their eild, their weight, their height, their grist,
   That rin for plates or purses
               Fu fleet this day."

To whisky plooks that brunt for wooks
   On town-guard soldiers' faces,
Their barber bauld his whittle crooks,
   An' scrapes them for the races:
Their stumps erst used to *filipegs*,
   Are dight in spatterdashes,
Whase barkent hides scarce fend their legs
   Frae weet, and weary plashes
               O' dirt that day.

"Come, hafe a care[5] (the captain cries),
   On guns your bagnets thraw;
Now mind your manual exercise,
   An' marsh down raw by raw."
And as they march he'll glowr about,
   Tent a' their cuts and scars:

---

4 **she'll craw kniefly in his crap**: i.e. she'll stick in his stomach when he cannot get rid of her later.
5 **hafe a care**: as in 'Hallow-Fair', Fergusson is imitating a Highland accent in these lines.

*Captain James Burnet,
last Captain of the City Guard, 1814*

'Mang them fell mony a gawsy snout
   Has gusht in birth-day wars,
                Wi blude that day.

Her Nanesel maun be carefu now,
   Nor maun she pe mislear'd,
Sin baxter lads hae seal'd a vow
   To skelp and clout the guard:[6]
I'm sure Auld Reikie kens o' nane
   That would be sorry at it,
Tho' they should dearly pay the kane,
   An' get their tails weel sautit[7]
                And sair thir days.

---

6 **clout the guard**: a journeyman baker had died on 19 July of wounds sustained during the riot on the King's birthday, and the bakers were out for revenge on the City Guard.

7 **get their tails weel sautit**: to "saut the tail" of someone is to punish them. Hence, here, "be well punished". For "pay the kane", see note to 'Mutual Complaint of Plainstanes and Causey'.

The tinkler billies i' the Bow [8]
   Are now less eident clinking,
As lang's their pith or siller dow,
   They're daffin, and they're drinking.
Bedown Leith-Walk what burrochs reel
   Of ilka trade and station,
That gar their wives an' childer feel
   Toom weyms for their libation
               O' drink thir days.

The browster wives thegither harl
   A' trash that they can fa on;
They rake the grounds o' ilka barrel,
   To profit by the lawen:
For weel wat they a skin leal het
   For drinking needs nae hire;
At drumly gear they take nae pet;
   Foul water slockens fire
               And drouth thir days.

They say, ill ale has been the deid
   O' mony a beirdly loun;
Then dinna gape like gleds wi greed
   To sweel hale bickers doun;
Gin Lord send mony ane the morn,
   They'll ban fu sair the time
That e'er they tootit aff the horn
   Which wambles thro' their weym
               Wi pain that day.

The Buchan bodies thro' the beach
   Their bunch of *Findrums*[9] cry,

---

8 **the Bow**: the West Bow, which ran from the Lawnmarket in a zig-zag to the Grassmarket, much more steeply than the present-day Victoria Street, was where many tinsmiths traded.
9 **Findrums**: Finnan haddies or speldings, small haddocks split and smoked. The name derives from the Kincardineshire fishing village

An' skirl out baul', in Norland speech,
　　"Gweed speldings, fa will buy?"
An', by my saul, they're nae wrang gear
　　To gust a stirrah's mou;
Weel staw'd wi them, he'll never spier
　　The price o' being fu
　　　　　　　Wi drink that day.

Now wyly wights at rowly-powl,[10]
　　An' flingin o' the dice,
Here brake the banes o' mony a sowl
　　Wi fa's upo' the ice:[11]
At first the gate seems fair an' straught,
　　So they had fairly til her;
But wow! in spite o' a' their maught,
　　They're rookit o' their siller
　　　　　　　An' gowd that day.

Around whare'er ye fling your een,
　　The haiks like wind are scourin;
Some chaises honest folk contain,
　　An' some hae mony a whure in;
Wi rose and lily, red and white,
　　They gie themselves sic fit airs,
Like Dian,[12] they will seem perfite;
　　But it's nae gowd that glitters
　　　　　　　Wi them thir days.

---

　　of Findon, the spelling Findrum from confusion with Findhorn in Morayshire.
10　**rowly-powl**: a game played at shows, where sticks were thrown to dislodge penny gingerbreads or other cakes mounted on pegs.
11　**ice**: i.e. gambling is as financially risky as ice.
12　**Dian**: Diana, the Roman goddess of hunting and woodlands. Fergusson may also be referring to the statue of Diana in the temple dedicated to her at Ephesus, which was one of the wonders of the ancient world. The silversmith Demetrius, whose trade depended on making shrines to Diana, organised a riot when St Paul denounced such statues as false gods. See the Bible, Acts, ch.xix.

The Lyon[13] here, wi open paw,
   May cleek in mony hunder,
Wha geck at Scotland and her law,
   His wyly talons under;
For ken, tho' Jamie's laws are auld,
   (Thanks to the wise recorder)
His Lyon yet roars loud and bauld,
   To had the Whigs in order
              Sae prime this day.

To town-guard drum of clangour clear,
   Baith men and steeds are raingit;
Some liveries red or yellow wear,
   And some are tartan spraingit:
And noo the red, the blue eenoo
   Bids fairest for the market;
But, ere the sport be done, I trou
   Their skins are gayly yarkit
              And peel'd thir days.

Siclike in Robinhood debates,[14]
   Whan twa chiels hae a pingle;
Eenow some cowlie gets his aits,
   An' dirt wi words they mingle,

---

13 **The Lyon**: the significance of this stanza lies with the Lyon King at Arms' right to punish the bearers of unauthorised arms. This was a particular issue with regard to gentlemen's carriages, and *The Weekly Magazine* had recently carried correspondence in which, broadly speaking, the Whigs thought a gentleman should be able to display whatever coat of arms he liked, while the Tories upheld Lord Lyon's right even to go so far as to seize a carriage if it bore unwarranted arms. Fergusson, as an anti-Unionist keen to protect Scottish tradition, sympathised with the latter school of thought. Here, he is also using the term "Whig" abusively in a much wider sense, referring to all lawbreakers, including petty thieves, disorderly people and other such scoundrels.

14 **Robinhood debates**: see note to 'Mutual Complaint of Plainstanes and Causey'.

Till up loups he, wi diction fu,
  There's lang and dreich contesting;
For now they're near the point in view;
  Now ten miles frae the question
      In hand that night.

The races owr, they hail the dools,[15]
  Wi drink o' a' kin-kind;
Great feck gae hirpling hame like fools,
  The cripple lead the blind.
May ne'er the canker o' the drink
  E'er make our spirits thrawart,
'Case we git therewitha' to wink
  Wi een as blue's a blawart[16]
      Wi straiks thir days!

Auld Reikie, July 21. [1773]

---

15 **hail the dools**: as explained by Allan Ramsay in a footnote to his poem 'Lucky Spence's Last Advice' (1718), "*Hale the Dools* is a Phrase used at Football, where the Party that gains the *Goal* or *Dool* is said to hail it or win the Game, and so draws the Stake". Fergusson uses it more loosely to mean "go all out".
16 **een as blue's a blawart**: i.e. may the evils of drink never put us in foul temper, or we'll get into fights and end up with eyes bruised as blue as harebells.

Ode to the Gowdspink

Frae fields whare Spring her sweets has blawn
Wi caller verdure owr the lawn,
The gowdspink comes in new attire,
The brawest 'mang the whistling choir,
That, ere the sun can clear his een,
Wi glib notes sain the simmer's green.

   Sure Nature herried mony a tree,
For spraings and bonny spats to thee:
Nae mair the rainbow can impart
Sic glowing ferlies o' her art,
Whase pencil wrought its freaks at will
On thee the sey-piece o' her skill.
Nae mair thro' straths in simmer dight
We seek the rose to bless our sight;
Or bid the bonny wa-flowers sprout
On yonder ruin's lofty snout.
Thy shining garments far outstrip
The cherries upo' Hebe's lip,
And fool[1] the tints that Nature chose
To busk and paint the crimson rose.

   'Mang man, wae's heart! we aften find
The brawest drest want peace of mind,
While he that gangs wi ragged coat
Is weel contentit wi his lot.
Whan wand wi glewy birdlime's set,
To steal far aff your dautit mate,
Blyth wad ye change your cleething gay

   First published in *The Weekly Magazine*, 12 August 1773.
1 **fool**: make look foolish.

In lieu of lav'rock's sober grey.
In vain thro' woods you sair may ban
Th' envious treachery of man,
That, wi your gowden glister taen,
Still hunts you on the simmer's plain,
And traps you 'mang the sudden fa's
O' winter's dreary dreepin snaws.
Now steekit frae the gowany field,
Frae ilka fav'rite houff and bield,
But mergh,² alas! to disengage
Your bonny bouk frae fettering cage,
Your free-born bosom beats in vain
For darling liberty again.
In window hung, how aft we see
Thee keek around at warblers free,
That carrol saft, and sweetly sing
Wi a' the blythness of the spring?
Like Tantalus³ they hing you here,
To spy the glories o' the year;
And tho' you're at the burnie's brink,
They downa suffer you to drink.

   Ah, Liberty! thou bonny dame,
How wildly wanton is thy stream,
Round whilk the birdies a' rejoice,
An' hail you wi a gratefu voice.
The gowdspink chatters joyous here,
And courts wi gleesome sangs his peer:
The mavis frae the new-bloom'd thorn

---

2 **but mergh**: without strength.
3 **Tantalus**: in Greek mythology, a Lydian king whose father was Zeus. He told the secrets of the gods to mortals, and was punished by being placed up to his chin in one of the rivers of Hades, with a fruit-laden tree just out of reach above his head. Whenever he tried to pluck the fruit, the waters receded and he failed to get any, which left him in agonies of thirst and hunger. From this story comes the word "tantalise".

Begins his lauds at ear'est morn;
And herd loun louping owr the grass,
Needs far less fleetching til his lass,
Than paughty damsels bred at courts,
Wha thraw their mous, and take the dorts:
But, reft of thee, fient flee we care
For a' that life ahint can spare.
The gowdspink, that sae lang has kend
Thy happy sweets (his wonted friend),
Her sad confinement ill can brook
In some dark chamber's dowy nook:
Tho' Mary's hand his neb supplies,
Unkend to hunger's painfu cries,
Ev'n beauty canna cheer the heart
Frae life, frae liberty apart;
For now we tyne its wonted lay,
Sae lightsome sweet, sae blythly gay.

   Thus Fortune aft a curse can gie,
To wyle us far frae liberty:
Then tent her siren smiles wha list,
I'll ne'er envy your girnal's grist;[4]
For whan fair freedom smiles nae mair,
Care I for life? Shame fa the hair;[5]
A field o'ergrown wi rankest stubble,
The essence of a paltry bubble.

North-Belton, Aug. 9. [1773]

---

4 **your girnal's grist**: the size of your meal-chest, i.e. your wealth.
5 **Shame fa the hair**: not so much as a hair.

To the Principal and Professors of the University of St Andrews, on their Superb Treat to Dr Samuel Johnson

St Andrews town may look right gawsy,
Nae grass will grow upon her cawsey,
Nor wa-flow'rs of a yellow dye,
Glowr dowy owr her ruins high,
Sin Samy's head weel pang'd wi lear
Has seen the *Alma Mater* there:
Regents,[1] my winsome billy boys!
'Bout him you've made an unco noise;
Nae doubt for him your bells wad clink,
To find him upon Eden's brink,[2]
An' a' things nicely set in order,
Wad kep him on the Fifan border:
I'se warrant now frae France an' Spain,
Baith cooks and scullions mony ane
Wad gar the pats an' kettles tingle
Around the college kitchen ingle,
To fleg frae a' your craigs the roup,
Wi reiking het and crieshy soup;
And snails and puddocks mony hunder

First published in *The Weekly Magazine*, 2 September 1773. Boswell, in his *Journal of a Tour to the Hebrides* (1786) notes, under Thursday, 19 August, "The professors entertained us with a very good dinner". Johnson had long wished to see St Andrews, and enjoyed his visit, although he was upset by the town's evident decay: "The kindness of the professors did not contribute to abate the uneasy remembrance of an university declining, a college alienated, and a church profaned and hastening to the ground." (*A Journey to the Western Islands of Scotland*, 1775)

1 **Regents**: professors.
2 **Eden's brink**: the river Eden flows through Fife and reaches the sea just west of St Andrews.

Wad beeking lie the hearth-stane under,
Wi roast and boil'd, an' a' kin kind,
To heat the body, cool the mind.

   But hear me, lads! gin I'd been there,
How I wad trimm'd the bill o' fare!
For ne'er sic surly wight as he
Had met wi sic respect frae me.
Mind ye what Sam, the lying loun!
Has in his Dictionar[3] laid doun?
That *aits* in England are a feast
To cow an' horse an' siccan beast,
While in Scots ground this growth was common
To gust the gab o' *man* an' *woman*.
Tak tent, ye Regents! then, an' hear
My list o' gudely hameil gear,
Sic as hae often rax'd the weym
O' blyther fallows mony time;
Mair hardy, souple, steeve an' swank,
Than ever stood on Samy's shank.

   Imprimis, then, a haggis fat,
Weel tottl'd in a seything pat,
Wi spice and ingans weel ca'd thro',
Had help'd to gust the stirrah's mou,
And plac'd itsel in truncher clean
Before the gilpy's glowrin een.

   Secundo, then, a gude sheep's head
Whase hide was singit, never flead,
And four black trotters cled wi girsle,
Bedown his throat had learn'd to hirsle.

---

[3] **Dictionar**: Johnson in his *Dictionary of the English Language* (1755) defined oats as "a grain, which in England is generally given to horses, but in Scotland supports the people".

What think ye neist, o' gude fat brose
To clag his ribs? a dainty dose!
And white and bloody puddins routh,
To gar the doctor skirl, "O Drouth!"
Whan he could never houp to merit
A cordial o' reaming claret,
But thraw his nose, and brize and pegh
Owr the contents o' sma ale quegh:
Then let his wisdom girn an' snarl
Owr a weel-toastit girdle farl,
An' learn, that maugre o' his wame,
Ill bairns are ay best heard at hame.

   Drummond, lang syne, o' Hawthornden,[4]
The wyliest an' best o' men,
Has gien you dishes ane or mae,
That wad ha' gar'd his grinders play,
Not to *roast beef*, old England's life,
But to the auld *east nook of Fife*,[5]
Whare Creilian crafts[6] could weel hae gien
Skate-rumples to hae clear'd his een;
Then neist, whan Samy's heart was faintin,
He'd lang'd for skate to mak him wanton.

   Ah! willawins, for Scotland noo,
Whan she maun stap ilk birky's mou
Wi eistacks, grown as 'tware in pet
In foreign land, or green-house het,

---

4 **Drummond o' Hawthornden**: Drummond's 'Polemo-Middinia' (see note to 'The King's Birth-Day in Edinburgh') opens with six lines which mention the varieties of seafood supplied by the fishing villages of the East Neuk of Fife.
5 **roast beef** and the **east nook of Fife**: Fergusson is alluding to two tunes, 'The Roast Beef of Old England', and 'East Neuk of Fife', which was published in Macgibbon's *Scots Tunes* (1755). For Macgibbon, see note to 'Elegy, on the Death of Scots Music'.
6 **Creilian crafts**: boats from Crail, ten miles down the coast from St Andrews.

When cog o' brose an' cutty spoon
Is a' our cottar childer's boon,
Wha thro' the week, till Sunday's speal,
Toil for pease-clods an' gude lang kail.
Devall then, Sirs, and never send
For daintiths to regale a friend,
Or, like a torch at baith ends burning,
Your house'll soon grow mirk and mourning.

   What's this I hear some cynic say?
Robin, ye loun! it's nae fair play;
Is there nae ither subject rife
To clap your thumb upon but Fife?
Gie owr, young man, you'll meet your corning,
Than caption waur, or charge o' horning;[7]
Some canker'd surly sour-mou'd carline[8]
Bred near the abbey o' Dumfarline,
Your shoulders yet may gie a lounder,
An' be of verse the mal-confounder.

   Come on, ye blades! but ere ye tulzie,
Or hack our flesh wi sword or gulzie,
Ne'er shaw your teeth, nor look like stink,
Nor owr an empty bicker blink:
What weets the wizen an' the weym,
Will mend your prose and heal my rhyme.

Edin. Sept. 1. [1773]

---

[7] **caption, horning**: a caption was a warrant for an arrest for debt, issued on behalf of a creditor. To be put to the horn was to be publicly proclaimed a rebel for non-payment of debts: letters of horning were a warrant issued in the name of the sovereign demanding payment, on penalty of being put to the horn.

[8] **sour-mou'd carline**: Fergusson had been challenged to a duel by a man from Dunfermline, who took offence at his derogatory remarks on Fife hospitality in his poem 'An Expedition to Fife and the Island of May'. He did not take up the challenge.

The Election

Nunc est bibendum, et bendere Bickerum magnum;
Cavete Town-guardum, Dougal Geddum atque Campbellum.[1]

Rejoice, ye burghers, ane an' a',
   Lang look't for's come at last;
Sair war your backs held to the wa
   Wi poortith an' wi fast:
Now ye may clap your wings an' craw,
   And gayly busk ilk feather,
For Deacon cocks hae pass'd a law
   To rax an' weet your leather
             Wi drink thir days.

"Haste Epps," quo John, "an' bring my gez,
   Take tent ye dinna't spulzie;
Last night the barber gae't a friz,
   An' straikit it wi ulzie.
Hae done your parritch, lassie Liz,
   Gie me my sark an' gravat;
I'se be as braw's the Deacon is
   Whan he taks *affidavit*
             O' *faith*[2] the day."

First published in *The Weekly Magazine*, 16 September 1773. The Edinburgh Town Council was made up of nineteen merchants and fourteen craftsmen, the Deacons of the "trades incorporations". Each of the trades (e.g. the goldsmiths, hammermen, skinners, surgeons, fleshers, tailors, baxters) put forward a leet of six candidates, which was then reduced to three by the Council, and from these the Deacons were chosen. The process was long, complicated and corrupt. Fergusson's poem concerns an early stage, the election of the Deacons and the accompanying dinner.

1 The macaronic motto translates: *Now for drinking and draining the big bicker; but beware the Town Guard, especially Dougals Ged and Campbell.*
2 **affidavit o' faith**: the oath of loyalty to the Crown and established religion.

"Whar's Johnny gaun," cries neebor Bess,
   "That he's sae gayly boden,
Wi new-kaim'd wig, weel syndet face,
   Silk hose, for³ hamely hodin?"
"Our Johnny's nae sma drink,⁴ you'll guess,
   He's trig as ony muir-cock,
An' forth to mak a Deacon, lass;
   He downa speak to poor fock
              Like us the day."

The coat ben-by i' the kist-nook,
   That's been this towmonth swarmin,
Is brought yence mair thereout to look,
   To fleg awa the vermin:
Menzies o' moths an' flaes are shook,
   An' i' the floor they howder,
Till in a birn beneath the crook
   They're singit wi a scowder
              To death that day.

The canty cobler quats his sta,
   His rozet an' his lingans;
His bouk has dree'd a sair, sair fa
   Frae meals o' bread an' ingans:
Now he's a pow o' wit an' law,
   An' taunts at soals an' heels;
To Walker's⁵ he can rin awa,
   There whang his creams an' jeels
              Wi life that day.

The lads in order tak their seat,
   (The deil may claw the clungest)

---

3 **for**: instead of.
4 **nae sma drink**: no insignificant person.
5 **Walker's**: Charles Walker's tavern in Writers' Court, on the north side of the High Street.

They stegh an' connach sae the meat,
   Their teeth mak mair than tongue haste:
Their claes sae cleanly dight an' feat,
   An' eke their craw-black beavers,
Like masters mows hae found the gate
     To tassels teugh wi slavers
          Fu lang that day.

The dinner done, for brandy strang
   They cry, to weet their thrapple,
To gar the stamack bide the bang,
   Nor wi its ladin grapple.
The grace is said – it's no owr lang;
   The claret reams in bells;
Quod Deacon, "Let the toast round gang,
   'Come, here's our noble sels
          Weel met the day.'"

"Weel's me o' drink," quo Cooper Will,
   "My barrel has been geyz'd ay,
An' has na gotten sic a fill
   Sin fu on Handsel-Teysday;
But makes-na,[6] now it's got a sweel,
   Ae gird I shanna cast, lad,
Or else I wish the horned deil
   May Will, wi kittle cast, dad
          To hell the day!"

The Magistrates fu wyly are,
   Their lamps are gayly blinking,
But they might as lieve burn elsewhere,
   Whan fock's blind fu wi drinking.
Our Deacon wadna ca a chair,

---

6 **But makes-na**: but it doesn't matter.

The foul ane[7] durst him na-say;
He took shanks' naig, but fient may care,
   He arselins kiss'd the cawsey
                Wi birr that night.

Weel loos me o' you, Souter Jock,
   For tricks ye buit[8] be trying,
Whan greapin for his ain bed-stock,
   He fa's whare Will's wife's lying.
Will coming hame wi ither fock,
   He saw Jock there before him:
Wi maister-laiglen, like a brock,
   He did wi stink maist smore him
                Fu strang that night.

Then wi a souple leathern whang
   He gart them fidge and girn ay:
"Faith, chiel, ye's no for naething gang,
   Gin ye maun reel my pirny."[9]
Syne wi a muckle alshin lang
   He brodit Maggie's hurdies;
An' 'cause he thought her i' the wrang,
   There pass'd nae bonny wordies
                'Mang them that night.

Now, had some laird his lady fand
   In sic unseemly courses,
It might hae loos'd the haly band,
   Wi lawsuits an' divorces;

---

7 **The foul ane**: the Devil.
8 **buit**: must (shortened form of *behove* or *behufe*).
9 **Gin ye maun reel my pirny**: to have "a ravelled pirn" (tangled bobbin) or "wind a bonnie pirn" is to create a problem, whether deliberately or unwittingly. (See David Murison, *Scots Saws*, Edinburgh 1981.) Hence, here: "If you're going to do me wrong, don't think you're going to get away with it."

But the neist day they a' shook hands,
    And ilka crack did sowder,
While Meg for drink her apron pawns,
    For a' the gudeman cow'd her
                Whan fu last night.

Glowr round the cawsey, up an' doun,
    What mobbing and what plotting!
Here politicians bribe a loun
    Against his saul for voting.
The gowd that inlakes half-a-croun
    Thir blades lug out to try them,[10]
They pouch the gowd, nor fash the toun
    For weights an' scales to weigh them
                Exact that day.

Then Deacons at the council stent
    To get themsels presentit:
For towmonths twa their saul is lent,
    For the town's gude indentit:
Lang's their debating thereanent,
    About *protests*[11] they're bauthrin;
While Sandy Fife, to mak content,
    On bells plays *Clout the Caudron*[12]
                To them that day.

Ye louns that troke in doctors' stuff,
    You'll now hae unco slaisters;[13]

---

10 **Thir blades lug out to try them**: i.e. these fellows bring out gold sovereigns half a crown light in value, to test allegiances.
11 **protests**: objections to the election's result or practices.
12 **Clout the Caudron**: a tune published in *Orpheus Caledonius*, Vol.II (1733). A set of bells in the tower of St Giles could be made to play various tunes by striking them by hand. Sandy Fife, presumably, was the name of the bellman.
13 **slaisters**: (unpalatable) mixtures, ointments.

Whan windy blaws their stamacks puff,
  They'll need baith pills an' plaisters;
For tho' ev'now they look right bluff,
  Sic drinks, ere hillocks meet,[14]
Will hap some Deacons in a truff,
  Inrow'd in the lang leet[15]
            O' death yon night.

Auld Reikie, Sept. 13. [1773]

---

14 **ere hillocks meet**: before too long.
15 **lang leet**: a nice reference to both the electoral procedures of the Council and death's leet, on which all would appear before being separated into the damned and the "elect".

ELEGY ON JOHN HOGG, LATE PORTER TO THE UNIVERSITY OF ST ANDREWS

Death, what's ado? The deil be licket,[1]
Or wi your stang, you ne'er had pricket,
Or our auld *Alma Mater* tricket
      O' poor John Hogg,
And trail'd him ben thro' your mirk wicket
      As dead's a log.

Now ilka glaikit scholar loun
May dander wae wi duddy goun;
Kate Kennedy[2] to dowy crune
      May mourn and clink,
And steeples o' St Andrew's toun
      To yird may sink.

Sin Pauly Tam[3] wi canker'd snout
First held the students in about,
To wear their claes as black as soot
      They ne'er had reason,
Till death John's haffit gae a clout,
      Sae out o' season.

    First published in *The Weekly Magazine*, 23 September 1773. John Hogg was popular with the students, although clearly old-fashioned and set in his ways. He had both property in the town and farmland outwith it. After his death his wife, Catherine Gourlay, married a Dean Landale, whom she also outlived.

1 **Death, what's ado? The deil be licket**: the sense here is, "Death, what's up? Things must be hellish..."
2 **Kate Kennedy**: a bell in the St Salvator's College steeple, dating from 1460, and supposedly named after the niece of Bishop Kennedy, founder of the college.
3 **Pauly Tam**: students' nickname for Thomas Tullidelph (d.1777), the College Principal, whose brand of discipline Fergusson himself had sampled (see Introduction). "Pauly" means either "pallid, sickly, stunted" or "flat-footed".

Whan regents[4] met at common schools,[5]
He taught auld Tam to hail the dools,[6]
And eident to rowe right the bools
    Like ony emmack;
He kept us a' within the rules
    Strict academic.

Heh! wha will tell the students now
To meet the Pauly cheek for chow,
Whan he, like frightsome wirrikow,
    Had wont to rail,
And set our stamacks in a lowe,
    Or we turn'd tail.

Ah, Johnny! aften did I grumble
Frae cozy bed fu ear' to tumble;
Whan art and part I'd been in some ill,
    Troth I was sweer,
His words they brodit like a wumill
    Frae ear to ear.

Whan I had been fu laith to rise,
John than begude to moralize:
"The tither nap, the sluggard cries,
    And turns him round;
Sae spake auld Solomon[7] the wise,
    Divine profound!"

---

4 **regents**: prior to the introduction of the professorial system around 1747, the regents were teachers who instructed a class in all subjects throughout the four years of study. Subsequently the title was applied to professors.
5 **common schools**: assemblies of the whole college before the Principal, who would dispense fines, suspensions and other punishments, and lecture the students on good behaviour.
6 **hail the dools**: hit the target. See note to 'Leith Races'.
7 **Solomon**: see the Bible, Proverbs, ch.6, 9–10: "How long wilt thou sleep, O sluggard? when wilt thou arise out of thy sleep? Yet a little sleep, a little slumber, a little folding of the hands to sleep."

Nae dominie, or wise Mess John,[8]
Was better lear'd in Solomon;
He cited proverbs one by one,
      Ilk vice to tame;
He gar'd ilk sinner sigh an' groan,
      And fear hell's flame.

"I hae nae meikle skill," quo he,
"In what you ca philosophy;
It tells that baith the earth and sea
      Rin round about;
Either the Bible tells a lee,
      Or you're a' out.

"It's i' the Psalms o' David[9] writ,
That this wide warld ne'er should flit,
But on the waters coshly sit
      Fu steeve and lasting;
An' was na he a head o' wit
      At sic contesting!"

On e'enings cauld wi glee we'd trudge
To heat our shins in Johnny's lodge;
The deil ane thought his bum to budge
      Wi siller on us:
To claw het pints we'd never grudge
      O' *molationis*.[10]

Say ye, red gowns! that aften here
Hae toasted bakes to Katie's beer,
Gin ere thir days hae had their peer,

---

8 **Mess John**: see note to 'The Farmer's Ingle'.
9 **Psalms o' David**: see the Bible, Psalm 24, 1–2.
10 **molationis**: macaronic Latin for a spirit distilled from molasses.

        Sae blyth, sae daft;
You'll ne'er again in life's career
        Sit ha'f sae saft.

Wi haffit locks, sae smooth and sleek,
John look'd like ony ancient Greek;
He was a Nazarene[11] a' the week,
        And doughtna tell out
A bawbee Scots to straik his cheek
        Tell Sunday fell out.

For John ay loo'd to turn the pence,
Thought poortith was a great offence:
"What recks tho' ye ken *mood* and *tense*?
        A hungry *weym*
For *gowd* wad wi them baith dispense
        At ony time.

"Ye ken what ails maun ay befall
The chiel that will be prodigal;
Whan wasted to the very spaul
        He turns his tusk,
For want o' comfort to his saul
        O' hungry husk."

Ye royit louns! Just do as he'd do;
For mony braw green shaw and meadow
He's left to cheer his dowy widow,
        His winsome Kate,
That to him prov'd a canny she-doo,
        Baith ear' and late.

---

11 **Nazarene**: a native of Nazareth, and the name given to early Christians. In fact, Fergusson means "Nazarite", a member of an Israelite sect who refrained from drink and let their hair grow long.

Dumfries

The gods sure in some canny hour
To bonny Nith hae taen a tour,
Whare bonny blinks the caller flow'r
    Beside the stream,
And sportive there hae shawn their pow'r
    In fairy dream.

Had Kirkhill[1] here but kent the gate,
The beauties on Dumfries that wait,
He'd never turn'd his canker'd pate
    Of satire keen,
Whan ilka thing's sae trig and feat,
    To cheer the een.

I ken the stirrah loo'd fu weel
Amang the drinking louns to reel,
An claret wine or porter sweel,
    Whilk he could get,
After a shank o' beer he'd peel,
    His craig to wet.

Marshall's an' *Bushby's*[2] then had fund
Some kitchen gude, to lay the grund,

  First published in *The Dumfries Weekly Magazine*, 28 September 1773. For the history of this poem, which was not reprinted in its correct form until 1930, see Matthew P. McDiarmid's note in *The Poems of Robert Fergusson* (Scottish Text Society, Vol.II, 1956), p.306.
1 **Kirkhill**: Charles Churchill (1731–64), English satirist, friend to John Wilkes whom he helped in publishing the *North Briton*, which attacked the Scots. His *Prophecy of Famine* (1763) is particularly fierce in its anti-Scottish sentiment.
2 **Marshall's an' Bushby's**: two wine-merchants and innkeepers in Dumfries.

And *Cheshire mites*³ had helped to hund
    And fley awa
The heart-scad an' a scud o' wind
    Frae stamack raw.

Had Horace liv'd, that pleasant sinner,
That loo'd gude wine to synd his dinner,
His muse tho' dowf, the deil be in her,
    She'd lous'd her tongue,
The drink could round Parnassus rin her
    In blythest sang.

Nae mair he'd sung to auld Maecenas,⁴
The blinking een o' bonny Venus,
His leave o' them he'd taen at anis
    For claret here,
Which Jove and a' his gods still rain us
    Frae year to year.

O Jove, man, gie's some orra pence,
Mair siller, an' a wie mair sense,
I'd bigg to you a rural spence,
    An' bide a' simmer,
An' cald frae saul and body fence
    With frequent brimmer.

---

3 **Cheshire mites**: Cheshire cheese well-ripened.
4 **Maecenas**: the Roman statesman (d.8 BC) who was the patron of poets including Horace and Virgil.

The Sitting of the Session

Phoebus, sair cow'd wi simmer's hight,[1]
Cours near the yird wi blinking light;
Cauld shaw the haughs, nae mair bedight
    Wi simmer's claes,
They heeze the heart[2] o' dowy wight
    That thro' them gaes.

Weel loos me o' you, Business, noo;
For ye'll weet mony a drouthy mou,
That's lang a eisning gane for you,
    Withouten fill
O' dribbles frae the gude *broun coo*,[3]
    Or Highland gill.

The Court o' Session, weel wat I,
Pits ilk chiel's whittle i' the pie,
Can criesh the slaw-gaun wheels whan dry,
    Till Session's done,
Tho' they'll gie mony a cheep and cry
    Or twalt o' June.[4]

Ye benders a', that dwall in joot,
You'll tak your liquor clean cap oot,

  First published in *The Weekly Magazine*, 4 November 1773. The Court of Session sat in winter from 12 November. See note to 'The Rising of the Session'.

1 **Phoebus, sair cow'd wi simmer's hight**: the sun, overawed by the height it reached in summer.
2 **They heeze the heart**: the apparently unlikely idea that the "cauld haughs" uplift some men's hearts is explained in the next stanza: the sitting of the Session means better business.
3 **broun coo**: a liquor vessel.
4 **Or twalt o' June**: before 12 June. The court did not sit between 12 March and this date, so business would be slow again in the intervening period.

Synd your moose-wabs⁵ wi reaming stoot,
    While ye hae cash,
And gar your cares a' tak the rout,
    An' thumb ne'er fash.

Rob Gibb's⁶ grey gizz, new frizzl'd fine,
Will white as ony snaw-ba shine;
Weel does he loo the *lawen coin*
    Whan dossied doun,
For whisky gills or dribbs of wine
    In cauld forenoon.

Bar-keepers now, at *outer door*,⁷
Tak tent as fock gang back and fore;
The fient ane there but pays his score,
    Nane wins toll-free,
Tho' ye've a *cause* the house before,
    Or agent be.

Gin ony here wi canker knocks,
And has na lous'd his siller pocks,
Ye need na think to fleetch or coax:
    "Come shaw's your gear;
Ae scabbit yew spills twenty flocks,⁸
    Ye's no be here."

Now at the door they'll raise a plea;
Crack on, my lads! – for flyting's free;
For gin ye should tongue-tackit be,
    The mair's the pity,

---

5 **moose-wabs**: cobwebs; here, dry phlegm in the throat.
6 **Rob Gibb**: see note to 'The Rising of the Session'.
7 **outer door**: see note above on Rob Gibb.
8 **Ae scabbit yew [yowe] spills twenty flocks**: one scabbed sheep ruins twenty flocks (a proverb found in various forms).

Whan scalding but and ben we see
    Pendente lite.[9]

The lawyer's skelfs,[10] and printer's presses,
Grane unco sair wi weighty cases;
The clark in toil his pleasure places,
    To thrive bedeen;
At five-hours' bell scribes shaw their faces,
    And rake their een.

The country fock to lawyers crook,
"Ah! Weel's me on your bonny bouk!
The benmost part o' my kist-nook
    I'll ripe for thee,
And willing ware my hindmost rook
    For my decree."

But law's a draw-well unco deep,
Withouten rim fock out to keep:
A donnart chiel, whan drunk, may dreep
    Fu sleely in,
But finds the gate baith stey and steep,
    Ere out he win.

---

9 **pendente lite**: pending the result of a plea.
10 **skelfs**: shelfs.

A Drink Eclogue : Landlady, Brandy and Whisky

On auld worm-eaten skelf, in cellar dunk,
Whare hearty benders syn'd their drouthy trunk,
Twa chappin bottles, pang'd wi liquor fu,
Brandy the tane, the tither Whisky blue,
Grew canker'd; for the twa war het within,
An' het-skinned fock to flyting soon begin.
The Frenchman fizz'd, and first wad foot the field,
While paughty Scotsman scorn'd to beenge or yield.

BRANDY
Black be your fa! ye cottar loun mislear'd,
Blawn by the porters, chairmen, city-guard;
Hae ye nae breeding, that you shaw your nose
Anent my sweetly gusted cordial dose?
I've been near pauky courts, and aften there
Hae ca'd hystericks frae the dowy fair;[1]
And courtiers aft gaed griening for my smack,
To gar them bauldly glowr, and gashly crack;
The priest, to bang mishaunters black, and cares,
Has sought me in his closet for his prayers.
What tig then takes the fates, that they can thole,
Thrawart to fix me in this weary hole,
Sair fash'd wi din, wi darkness, and wi stinks,
Whare cheery day-light thro' the mirk ne'er blinks?

WHISKY
But ye maun be content, and maunna rue,
Tho' erst ye've bizz'd in bonny madam's mou;

First published in *The Weekly Magazine*, 11 November 1773.
1 **Hae ca'd hystericks frae the dowy fair:** have driven hysterical fits from dispirited/ailing/weakly members of the fair sex.

Wi thoughts like thae your heart may sairly dunt;
The warld's now chang'd, it's no like use and wont;
For here, wae's me! there's nouther lord nor laird
Come to get heart-scad frae their stamack skair'd;
Nae mair your courtier louns will shaw their face,
For they glowr eery at a friend's disgrace;
But heeze your heart up – whan at court you hear
The patriot's thrapple wat wi reaming beer;
Whan chairman, weary wi his daily gain,
Can syn' his whistle wi the clear champaign;
Be hopefu, for the time will soon rowe round,
Whan you'll nae langer dwall beneath the ground.

BRANDY
Wanwordy gowk! did I sae aften shine
Wi gowden glister thro' the crystal fine,
To thole your taunts, that seenil hae been seen
Awa frae luggie, quegh, or truncher treen;
Gif honour wad but lat, a challenge should
Twin[2] ye o' Highland tongue and Highland blude;
Wi cairds like thee I scorn to fyle my thoum,
For gentle spirits gentle breeding doom.[3]

WHISKY
Truly I think it right you get your amis,
Your high heart humbled amang common drams:
Braw days for you, whan fools newfangle fain,
Like ither countries better than their ain,
For there ye never saw sic chancy days,
Sic balls, assemblies, operas, or plays:
Hame-owr lang syne you hae been blyth to pack
Your a' upon a sarkless soldier's back;

---

2 **twin**: deprive.
3 **gentle spirits gentle breeding doom**: gentility necessitates genteel manners (therefore honour does not allow me to trouble myself over tinkers like you).

For you thir lads, as weel-lear'd trav'lers tell,
Had sell'd their sarks, gin sarks they'd had to sell.
   But worth gets poortith an' black burning shame,
To draunt and drivel out a life at hame.
Alake! the byword's owr weel kend throughoot,
"Prophets at hame are held in nae repute";
Sae fair'st wi me, tho' I can heat the skin,
And set the saul upon a merry pin,
Yet I am hameil, there's the sour mischance!
I'm no frae Turkey, Italy, or France;
For now our gentles' gabs are grown sae nice,
At thee they toot, an' never spier my price:
Witness – for thee they hight their tenants' rent,
And fill their lands wi poortith, discontent;
Gar them owr seas for cheaper mailins hunt,
An' leave their ain as bare's the Cairn-o'-mount.[4]

BRANDY
Tho' lairds take toothfu's o' my warming sap,
This dwynes nor tenants' gear, nor cows their crap:
For love to you, there's mony a tenant gaes
Bare-ars'd and barefoot owr the Highland braes;
For you nae mair the thrifty gudewife sees
Her lasses kirn, or birze the dainty cheese;
Crummie[5] nae mair for Jenny's hand will crune
Wi milkness dreeping frae her teats adoun;
For you owr ear' the ox his fate partakes,
And fa's a victim to the bludey aix.

WHISKY
Wha is't that gars the greedy bankers prieve
The maiden's tocher, but[6] the maiden's leave?

---

[4] **Cairn-o'-mount:** a hill on the road between Fettercairn and Banchory.
[5] **Crummie:** pet name for a cow. See note to 'The Farmer's Ingle'.
[6] **but:** without.

By you when spulzied o' her charming pose
She tholes in turn the taunt o' cauldrife joes;
Wi skelps like this fock sit but seenil down
To wether-gammond or how-towdy brown;
Sair dung wi dule, and fley'd for coming debt,
They gar their mou-bits wi their incomes mett,
Content eneugh gif they hae wherewithal
Scrimply to tack their body and their saul.

BRANDY
Frae some poor poet, owr as poor a pot,
Ye've lear'd to crack sae crouse, ye haveril Scot!
Or burgher politician, that embrues
His tongue in thee, and reads the claiking news;
But wae's heart for you! that for ay maun dwell
In poet's garret, or in chairman's cell,
While I shall yet on bien-clad tables stand,
Bowden wi a' the daintiths o' the land.

WHISKY
Troth I hae been ere now the poet's flame,
And heez'd his sangs to mony blythsome theme.
Wha was't gar'd Allie's[7] chaunter chirm fu clear,
Life to the saul, and music to the ear?
Nae stream but kens, and can repeat the lay
To shepherds streekit on the simmer brae,
Wha to their whistle wi the lav'rock bang,
To wauken flocks the rural fields amang.

BRANDY
But here's the browster wife, and she can tell
Wha's win[8] the day, and wha should wear the bell:
Hae done your din, an' lat her judgment join
In final verdict 'twixt your pley and mine.

---

7 **Allie**: Allan Ramsay.
8 **Wha's win**: who will win.

LANDLADY
In days o' yore I could my living prize,
Nor faush'd wi dolefu gaugers or excise;
But now-a-days we're blyth to lear the thrift,
Our heads 'boon licence and excise to lift:
Inlakes o' brandy we can soon supply
By whisky tinctur'd wi the saffron's dye.
  Will you your breeding threep, ye mongrel loun!
Frae hame-bred liquor dy'd to colour broun?
So flunky braw, whan drest in master's claes,
Struts to Auld Reikie's cross on sunny days,
Till some auld comrade, ablins out o' place,
Near the vain upstart shaws his meagre face;
Bumbaz'd he loups frae sight, and jooks his ken,
Fley'd to be seen amang the tassel'd train.[9]

---

9 **the tassel'd train**: i.e. the disordered or ragged set tagging on behind.

To My Auld Breeks

Now gae your wa's – Tho' anes as gude
As ever happit flesh and blude,
Yet part we maun – The case sae hard is,
Amang the writers and the bardies,
That lang they'll brook the auld I trou,
Or neibours cry, "Weel brook the new";[1]
Still making tight wi tither steek,
The tither hole, the tither eik,
To bang the birr o' winter's anger,
And had the hurdies out o' langer.[2]

   Siclike some weary wight will fill
His kyte wi drogs frae doctor's bill,
Thinking to tack the tither year
To life, and look baith hale an' fier,
Till at the lang-run death dirks in,
To birze his saul ayont his skin.

   You needna wag your duds o' clouts,
Nor fa into your dorty pouts,
To think that erst you've hain'd my tail
Frae wind and weet, frae snaw and hail,
And for reward, whan bald and hummil,
Frae garret high to dree a tumble.
For you I car'd, as lang's ye dow'd
Be lin'd wi siller or wi gowd:

First published in *The Weekly Magazine*, 25 November 1773.
1 **Weel brook the new**: congratulations on the new clothes.
2 **had the hurdies out o' langer**: to "haud someone oot o' langour" is to keep their spirits up. Hence, here, "keep the backside from distress".

Now to befriend, it wad be folly,
Your raggit hide an' pouches holey;
For wha but kens a poet's placks
Get mony weary flaws an' cracks,
And canna thole to hae them tint,
As he sae seenil sees the mint?
Yet round the warld keek and see,
That ithers fare as ill as thee;
For weel we loo the chiel we think
Can get us tick, or gie us drink,
Till o' his purse we've seen the bottom,
Then we despise, and hae forgot him.

Yet gratefu hearts, to make amends,
Will ay be sorry for their friends,
And I for thee – As mony a time
Wi you I've speel'd the braes o' rime,
Whare for the time the Muse ne'er cares
For siller, or sic guilefu wares,
Wi whilk we drumly grow, and crabbit,
Dour, capernoited, thrawin gabbit,[3]
And brither, sister, friend and fae,
Without remeid of kindred, slay.

You've seen me round the bickers reel
Wi heart as hale as temper'd steel,
And face sae apen, free and blyth,
Nor thought that sorrow there could kyth;
But the neist mament this was lost,
Like gowan in December's frost.

Could *Prick-the-louse*[4] but be sae handy
To make the breeks and claes to stand ay,

---

3 **thrawin gabbit**: thrawn-gabbit, sour-mouthed or perverse.
4 **Prick-the-louse**: contemptuous name for a tailor.

Thro' thick and thin wi you I'd dash on,
Nor mind the folly of the fashion:
But, hegh! the times' *vicissitudo*
Gars ither breeks decay as you do.
Thae Macaronies, braw and windy,
Maun fail – *Sic transit gloria mundi!*

   Now speed you to some madam's chaumer,
That but an' ben rings dule an' claumer,
Ask her, in kindness, if she seeks
In hidling ways to wear the breeks?
Safe you may dwall, tho' mould and motty,
Beneath the veil o' under coatie,
For this mair faults nor yours can screen
Frae lover's quickest sense, his een.

   Or if some bard, in lucky times,
Should profit meikle by his rhymes,
And pace awa, wi smirky face,
In siller or in gowden lace,
Glowr in his face, like spectre gaunt,
Remind him o' his former want,
To cow his daffin and his pleasure,
And gar him live within the measure.

   So Philip,[5] it is said, who would ring
Owr Macedon a just and gude king,
Fearing that power might plume his feather,

---

[5] **Philip**: Matthew P. McDiarmid notes that the closest reference he could find to the tradition as presented by Fergusson occurs in Thomas Leland's *The History of the Life and Reign of Philip King of Macedon* (London, 1758), where it is written that "every day, before he gave an audience, an officer was employed to remind him in form, that HE WAS MORTAL." See McDiarmid, *The Poems of Robert Fergusson* (Scottish Text Society, Vol.II, 1956), p.314.

And bid him stretch beyond the tether,
Ilk morning to his lug wad ca
A tiny servant o' his ha,
To tell him to improve his span,
For Philip was, like him, a man.

Rob. Fergusson's Last Will

While sober folks, in humble prose,
Estate, and goods, and gear dispose,
A poet surely may disperse
His moveables in doggrel verse;
And fearing death my blood will fast chill,
I hereby constitute my last will.
   Then wit ye me to have made o'er
To Nature my poetic lore;
To her I give and grant the freedom
Of paying to the bards who need 'em
As many talents as she gave,
When I became the Muses' slave.
   Thanks to the gods, who made me poor!
No lukewarm friends molest my door,
Who always shew a busy care
For being legatee or heir:
Of this stamp none will ever follow
The youth that's favour'd by Apollo.
   But to those few who know my case,
Nor thought a *poet's friend* disgrace,
The following trifles I bequeath,
And leave them with my kindest breath;

First published in *The Weekly Magazine*, 25 November 1773. Matthew P. McDiarmid points out that "the poetic inventory – usually in the testamentary form – is ... a literary joke of some antiquity", but that Fergusson may have got the idea from verses published in the previous week's magazine, entitled 'An Inventory of Dr Swift's Goods, upon lending his House to the Bishop of M. Not printed in his works.' See *The Poems of Robert Fergusson* (Scottish Text Society, Vol.II, 1956), p.314. Although comic, this poem is tinged with a solemnity which reflects the illness and depression into which the poet was already sinking. The last poem of his to be published in *The Weekly Magazine* appeared a month later, the 'Codicile to Rob. Fergusson's Last Will'. It is a weary extension of the same joke, and further evidence of his decline.

Nor will I burden them with payment
Of debts incurr'd, or coffin raiment,
As yet 'twas never my intent
To pass an Irish compliment.
   To Jamie Rae,[1] who oft *jocosus*
With me partook of cheering doses,
I leave my snuff-box, to regale
His senses after drowsy meal,
And wake remembrance of a friend
Who lov'd him to his latter end:
But if this pledge should make him sorry,
And argue like *memento mori*,
He may bequeath't 'mong stubborn fellows,
To all the finer feelings callous,
Who think that parting breath's a sneeze
To set sensations all at ease.
   To Oliphant,[2] my friend, I legate
Those scrolls poetic which he may get,
With ample freedom to correct
Those writs I ne'er could retrospect,
With power to him and his succession
To print and sell a new impression:
And here I fix on Ossian's Head,[3]
A domicile for Doric reed,[4]
With as much power *ad Musæ bona*,
As I *in propria persona*.[5]
   To Hamilton I give the task

---

1 **Jamie Rae**: Rae and the John Hamilton mentioned later in the poem were both "procurators" or solicitors at the lower courts, and close friends of Fergusson.
2 **Oliphant**: a bookseller friend, and apparently also a poet.
3 **Ossian's Head**: Alexander Kincaid's press, which had printed Fergusson's separate edition of 'Auld Reikie'.
4 **Doric reed**: verse in Scots as opposed to that in English.
5 **ad Musæ bona**: the sense is, "I invest Ossian's Head with as much power with regard to the goods of the Muse as I would have in my own personal property."

Outstanding debts to crave and ask;
And that my Muse he may not dub ill,
For loading him with so much trouble,
My debts I leave him *singulatim*,[6]
As they are mostly *desperatim*.[7]

   To Woods,[8] whose genius can provoke
His passions to the bowl or sock,[9]
For love to thee, and to the nine,[10]
Be my immortal Shakespeare thine:
Here may you thro' the alleys turn,
Where Falstaff laughs, where heroes mourn,
And boldly catch the glowing fire
That dwells in raptures on his lyre.

   Now at my dirge (if dirge there be!),
Due to the Muse and poetry,
Let Hutcheson[11] attend, for none is
More fit to guide the ceremonies;
As I in health with him would often
This clay-built mansion wash and soften,
So let my friends with him partake
The gen'rous wine at dirge or wake –

   And I consent to registration
Of this my will for preservation,
That patent it may be, and seen
In Walter's Weekly Magazine.
Witness whereof, these presents wrote are
By William Blair, the public notar,
And, for the tremor of my hand,
Are sign'd by him at my command.

                    R.F. † his Mark.

---

6 **singulatim**: one at a time.
7 **desperatim**: hopeless.
8 **Woods**: William Woods, an actor friend.
9 **sock**: soak (i.e. drinking-bout).
10 **the nine**: the Muses.
11 **Hutcheson**: James Hutcheson, a tavern-keeper, and probably the same man who went by the name of Sir Whisky in the Cape Club.

HORACE, ODE XI. LIB I

Ne'er fash your thumb what gods decree
To be the weird o' you or me,
Nor deal in cantrup's kittle cunning
To spier how fast your days are running,
But patient lippen for the best,
Nor be in dowy thought opprest,
Whether we see mair winters come
Than this that spits wi canker'd foam.

  Now moisten weel your geyzen'd waas
Wi couthy friends and hearty blaws;
Ne'er lat your hope owrgang your days,
For eild and thraldom never stays;[1]
The day looks gash, toot aff your horn,
Nor care yae strae about the morn.

First published in *Poems on Various Subjects, By Robert Fergusson, Part II* (Walter and Thomas Ruddiman, Edinburgh, 1779), under 'Posthumous Pieces'. This is the ode of Horace's which contains the famous line "Carpe diem, quam minimum credula postero" (seize the day, put no trust in the future) which becomes Fergusson's last two lines.

1 **stays**: stops coming.

The Author's Life

My life is like the flowing stream
That glides where summer's beauties teem,
Meets all the riches of the gale
That on its watry bosom sail,
And wanders 'midst Elysian groves
Thro' all the haunts that fancy loves.
   May I, when drooping days decline,
And 'gainst those genial streams combine,
The winter's sad decay forsake,
And center in my parent lake.

First published in *Poems on Various Subjects, By Robert Fergusson, Part II* (Walter and Thomas Ruddiman, Edinburgh, 1779), under 'Posthumous Pieces'.

On Night

Now murky shades surround the pole;
Darkness lords without controul;
To the notes of buzzing owl
Lions roar, and tygers howl,
Fright'ning from their azure shrine
Stars that wont in orbs to shine:
Now the sailor's storm-tost bark
Knows no blest celestial mark,
While, in the briny troubled deep,
Dolphins change their sport for sleep:
Ghosts, and frightful spectres gaunt,
Church-yards' dreary footsteps haunt,
And brush, with wither'd arms, the dews
That fall upon the drooping yews.

Published in *A Collection of English Prose and Verse, for the Use of Schools. By Arthur Masson, M.A.* (Edinburgh, 1788), and then in *The Poetical Works of Robert Fergusson, with the Life of the Author*, edited by David Irving (Glasgow, 1800).

Job, Chapter III, Paraphrased

Perish the fatal day when I was born,
The night with dreary darkness be forlorn;
The loathed, hateful, and lamented night
When Job, 'twas told, had first perceiv'd the light;
Let it be dark, nor let the God on high
Regard it with the favour of his eye;
Let blackest darkness and death's awful shade
Stain it, and make the trembling earth afraid;
Be it not join'd unto the varying year,
Nor to the fleeting months in swift career.
Lo! Let the night in solitude's dismay
Be dumb to joy, and waste in gloom away;
On it may twilight stars be never known;
Light let it wish for, Lord! but give it none;
Curse it let them who curse the passing day,
And to the voice of mourning raise the lay;
Nor ever be the face of dawning seen
To ope its lustre on th' enamel'd green;
Because it seal'd not up my mother's womb,
Nor hid from me the sorrows doom'd to come.
Why have I not from mother's womb expir'd?
My life resign'd when life was first requir'd?
Why did supporting knees prevent my death,
Or suckling breasts sustain my infant breath?
For now my soul with quiet had been blest,
With kings and counsellors of earth at rest,
Who bade the house of desolation rise,
And awful ruin strike tyrannic eyes,
Or with the princes unto whom were told

First published in *Poems on Various Subjects, By Robert Fergusson, Part II* (Walter and Thomas Ruddiman, Edinburgh, 1779), under 'Posthumous Pieces'.

Rich store of silver and corrupting gold;
Or, as untimely birth, I had not been,
Like infant who the light hath never seen;
For there the wicked from their trouble cease,
And there the weary find their lasting peace;
There the poor prisoners together rest,
Nor by the hand of injury opprest;
The small and great together mingl'd are,
And free the servant from his master there;
Say, Wherefore has an over-bounteous heaven
Light to the comfortless and wretched given?[1]
Why should the troubl'd and oppress'd in soul
Fret over restless life's unsettled bowl,
Who long for death, who lists not to their pray'r,
And dig as for the treasures hid afar;
Who with excess of joy are blest and glad,
Rejoic'd when in the tomb of silence laid?
Why then is grateful light bestow'd on man,
Whose life is darkness, all his days a span?
For ere the morn return'd my sighing came,
My mourning pour'd out as the mountain stream;
Wild visag'd fear, with sorrow-mingled eye,
And wan destruction piteous stared me nigh;
For though nor rest nor safety blest my soul,
New trouble came, new darkness, new controul.

---

[1] **Say, Wherefore has an over-bounteous heaven light to the comfortless and wretched given?**: these lines were quoted by Burns three months before his death, in a letter to George Thomson in April 1796: "I look on the vernal day, & say with poor Fergusson…"

GLOSSARY

(Abdn) = Aberdeenshire, (Gael) = Gaelic, (AG) = variant spellings in the poems 'To R. Fergusson' and 'To Andrew Gray'

a', all
abien (AG), see **aboon**
ablins, perhaps
aboon, above
ae, one
aff, off
afley'd, afraid
aft(en), oft(en)
afterhend, afterwards
agains, against
aik, ache
aik, oak
ain, own
air, early
air-cock, weather-cock
airth, direction
aiten, oaten
aits, oats
aith, oath
aix, axe
alake, alack, alas
alshin, awl
amang, among
amis, alms, i.e. just deserts
amry, cupboard
an', and
an, if
ane, one
anent, alongside
anes, anis, once
anither, another
antrin, rare, different
apen, open
aqua vitae, whisky
arselins, on/with his arse
aucht, eight

auld, old
auld-farran(t), wise, witty
Auld Nick, the Devil
awa, away
ay, always, ever
ayont, beyond

ba, ball
back-gaun, needy, failing
bagnet, bayonet
bairn, child
baith, both
ban, curse
bane, bone
bang, overcome, beat, strive
bang, crowd, stuff
barkent, hardened
barras, enclosure
bassie, pet name for a (usually old) horse
baudrins, pussy
bauk, unploughed strip of land
bauld, bold
bauthrin, bothering
bawbee, halfpenny
bawk, bat
baxter, baker
bear seed, barley-sowing time
bedeckit, bedecked, adorned
bedeen, at once
bedight, arrayed
bedown, down
beek, warm
beenge, bow, fawn
begude, began
behad, behold

beirdly, strong
ben, through, within
benders, drinkers
benmost, innermost
bent, grass
bents, grasslands
betaken, betoken
beted, befell
bicker, drinking-vessel
bield, shelter
bien, comfortable, cosy
bienly, comfortably, prosperously
bigg, build
biggin(g), building
billie, billy, lad, comrade
bink, shelf
binna, be not
birk, birken, birch
birkie/birky, fellow
birl, spin, move rapidly
birn, burden; **in a birn**, all together
birr, force
birsel, scorch
birze, bruise, squeeze
bisket, breast
bizz, buzz, hiss, foam
bizzin(g), foaming, burning, dry
blate, reluctant, shy
blaw, blow, bloom
blaw, draught, pull (of liquor)
blawart, harebell, bluebell
bleer, flicker
bleering, dimming
bleid (AG), blood
blink, glance, shine
blinkit, drunk
blinks, rays, moments of sunshine
blude, blood
blyth, blithe, happy
boden, provided, supplied
bodle, small copper coin
bogle, frightening ghost
bon-grace, straw bonnet
bools, bowls
bore, hole
Boreas, the North Wind
Borrowstown, borough town
bougil, bugle, cock-crow
bouk, body, self
bourach, heap, mass, cluster
bowden, swollen, laden
bowie, ale-barrel
brae, hill
braid, broad
braw, fine, excellent
breid, bread
brig, bridge
brimmer, drinking-vessel full to the brim
brither, brother
brize, puff
broachie, broach
brock, badger
brodit, goaded, prodded
broo, brow
brook, bear, enjoy the use of
broom-thackit, broom-thatched
brose, oat or pease-meal, mixed with boiling water, salt, butter etc.
browst(er), brew(er)
brulzie, fight, brawl
brunt, burned
buit, must
bum, drone, play
bumbazed, surprised, embarrassed

burroch, see **bourach**
busk, dress, deck
buss, bush
but and ben, outside and within
bygane, past
byke, bees' nest
byword, proverb

ca, call
ca, drive, knock
ca'd thro', stirred through
cadgie, happy
cadie, messenger
caird, gipsy, tinker
cald, see **cauld**
caldrife, see **cauldrife**
callant, lad
caller, fresh, cool
canker('d), ill-temper(ed)
canna, cannot
cannily, happily, gently
canny, lucky, clever
cantrup, magic spell, trick
canty, pleasant, cheery
cap, cup
capernoited, capernoity, irritable
carle, fellow
carline, old wife
cassen, cast
caudron, caldron
cauld, cold
cauldrife, cold
causey, cawsey, street
chancy, lucky
chap, knock, break up
chapman, pedlar
chappin, chopin, liquid measure of about 1.5 pints
charot, carriage

chaumer, chamber
chaunter, chanter
chawmir, see **chaumer**
chiel(d), chap, fellow
childer, children
chirm, chirp, warble
chopies, shops
chow, chew; **cheek for chow**, cheek by jowl
clack, chatter, clatter
claes, clothes
clag, clog, stick to
claik, see **clack**
claith, cloth
clamihewit, a blow
clamp, heavy footstep, clump
clarty, filthy
clash(es), gossip, rumour
clatter, chatter
claumer, clamour
claver, clover
cled, clad
cleed, clothe
cleedin(g), cleething, clothing
cleek, seize, hook
cleugh, rock, crag
clink, cash
clink, ring
clitter-clatter, nonsense
clour, strike, batter
clouted, patched
clungest, hungriest
coaties, petticoats
coble, small flat-bottomed fishing-boat
cod, pillow
codlin, codling
codroch, idle, low-class
coft, bought
cog, cogie, wooden dish

connach, demolish, devour
coof, fool
corbie, raven
corning (meet your corning), get your deserts
corp, corpse
cosh, snug, cosy
cottar, cottager
coup, exchange
cour, cower, crouch
couter, iron cutter in front of a ploughshare
couth, friendly, cosy
couthie, couthy, snug, friendly
cowlie, fellow (contemptuous)
cowr, recover from
crabbit, harsh, ill-tempered
crack, boast, talk
craig, neck, throat
craig, rock, crag
crap, belly
crap, crept
crap, crop
craw, crow
crazy, cracked, damaged
creesh, slap, thrashing
criesh, grease
crook, twist, bend, bow
croun, crown
croup(in), croak(ing)
crouse, bold
crously, arrogantly
crowdy-meal, porridge
cruizy, oil-lamp
crune, bellow, sing in lament
cuisser, stallion
cull, fool
cunzied, coined, made
cutty spoon, short-handled spoon

cutty-stool, kirk stool of repentance
cutty stoup, tankard

dad, dash
daff, act foolishly, make merry
daffin, making merry
daintith, delicacy
dander, wander, stroll
dang, see **ding**
darna, dare not
daub, dab, expert
daut, pet, spoil
dautit, spoilt, beloved
daw, dawn
dead-deal, board for laying out a corpse
deas, wooden settle
deave, deafen
deid, dead, death
deil, devil
dern, hidden, secret
devall, desist, cease
dight, arrayed
dighted, finished off
dighting, cleaning, sifting of grain
ding, strike, beat, knock
dinlin, rattling
dinna, do not
dinsome, noisy
dint, effect
dirk, slink, lurk
disna, does not
divet, divot, turf
dockan, dock
doil'd, wearied
doitet, crazed, daft
dolefu, doleful
dominie, schoolmaster

donnart, stupid
dool, trouble, sorrow
doolfu, troublesome
dorts, sulks
dorty, sulky
dosen, doze, drowse
dossie doun, toss down
dought, could
doughtna, see **downa**
douk, duck
doun, down
doup, bum, buttocks
dour, grim
dout, doubt
dow, could, enable
dow, fade, wither
dowf, sad, melancholy
dowie, dowy, gloomy, sad
downa, will not, would not, may not, could not
dowp, backside
dowy, see **dowie**
dragled, drenched, bedraggled
drap, drop
draunt, drag, drawl
dree, endure
dreep, drip
dreep, descend (from a rim etc.) by letting oneself down to the full stretch of the arms and dropping
dreepin(g), dripping
dreich, wearisome
dreid, dread, fear
dribb, drop
drog, drug
droukit, soaked
drouth(y), thirst(y)
drumly, confused, troubled, impure
dub(b)s, puddles

duddies, shabby clothes
duds, clothes
dule (AG), see **dool**
dun(s), demand(s) for payment
dung, struck, done in
dunk, damp
dunt, blow, beat
dwall, dwell
dwyne, fade, decline, reduce

ear', early
ebon, ebony
Edina, Edinburgh
ee(n), eye(s)
e'en, even, evening
eenoo, eenow, even now
eftsoons, soon enough
eident, busy, diligent
eik, patch
eikit, added
eild, (old) age
eisning, desiring (especially of a cow for the bull)
eistacks, dainties
eith, eithly, easy, easily
eke, also
eldin, fuel
ell, a measure of length
emmack, ant
eneugh, enough

fa (Abdn), who
fa, fall, befall
fa owr, fall asleep
faan, fallen
fadge, bannock, flat loaf
fae, foe
fain, glad, gladly, keen
fairin, gift or food at a fair
fairn-year, last year

fair'st, fares
fald, fold, leaf, sheepfold, enclosure
fallow, fellow
fand, see **fund**
farden, farthing
fareweel, farewell
farl, see **girdle farl**
farran, see **auld farran(t)**
farrer, farther
fash, trouble, bother; **ne'er fash your thumb**, not be put out
faugh'd, fallowed
faught, fight
fauld, see **fald**
faush, see **fash**
fawn, fallen
fearn, fern
feat, trim, pretty
feck, plenty, a good quantity; **feckly (maist feckly)**, for the most part
feckless, feeble, powerless
feg, fig
fegs, in truth, truly
fell, supply
fend, protect
fenzy, feign, pretend
ferly, wonder, mystery
ferra coo, milkless cow
fidge, twitch, jerk
fiend haet awa, devil a bit of it!, not a thing!
fient (the fient), scarcely
fient flee, not a thing
fier, healthy
fike, fuss
filipegs (Gael), kilts
finger-nebbs, fingertips
fint (AG), see **fient**

fire-flaught, lightning
fitt, foot
flae, flay
flae, flea
flaff, flutter
flead, flayed
flee, fly
fleetch, flatter, beguile
fleg, frighten
fleuk, flounder
fley, frighten, put to flight
flit, move, shift
flung, jilted, baffled, deceived
flyte, wrangle, scold
flyting, scolding
fock, folk
forfoughen, worn out
forgether, gather together
forseeth (Abdn), forsooth
forspeak, presage
fou, fu, full, drunk
fou (AG), how
fouk, folk
fousom, over-rich, filling
fouth, plenty
foy, farewell feast
frae, from
freaks, tricks
fu, full, drunk
fund, found
fusion, energy, capability
fyle, defile, dirty

gab, mouth
gabbies, mouths
gabblin, speaking
gae, gave
gae, go
gamon, leg
gane, gone

gang, go
gar, cause, make, force
gardies, fists raised to fight
gash, bright
gash, talk
gashly, freely
gate, bearing, way
gaudsmen, ploughmen
gaugers, excisemen
gaunt, yawn
gaw, gall, bile
gawn, going
gawsy, handsome, showy
geck, mock
geed (AG), see **gweed**
geyz'd, geyzen'd, see **gizzen'd**
gez, wig
gezy-maker, wig-maker
ghaist, ghost
gie, gien, give, given
gif, if
gilpy, rascal
gimcrack, fancy
gimmer, gossip, crony
gin, if
gird, hoop
girdle farl, quarter oatcake baked on a girdle
girn, grimace, complain
girnal, meal-chest
girsle, gristle
gizz, wig
gizzen, dry up, grow thirsty
gizzen'd, dried out
glaikit, glakit, silly, daft
glamer, glamour, enchantment
gled, kite, greedy person
gleg, keen, quick
glent, gleam
gleyb, glebe, cultivated soil

gloamin(g), gloaming, twilight
glore, glory
glowr, gaze, stare, look stern
gowan, daisy
gowd(en), gold(en)
gowdspink, goldfinch
gowk, cuckoo, fool
gowpin, double-handful
graith, gear, stuff, apparel
grane, groan
grassum gift, fee paid to a landlord
gravat, cravat
greapin, groping
gree (**bear the gree**), prize (carry off the prize)
'gree, agree
greet, weep, cry
grien, yearn (for)
grist, size
groat, small coin
gruntle, grunt
gudame, granny
gudeman, master of the house, husband
gudewife, mistress of the house, wife
guide, control, direct
gulzie, knife
gust(it), flavour(ed)
gust (**the gab**), treat (the mouth)
gusty, tasty
gutcher, grandfather, ancestor
gweed (Abdn), good

habuliments, attire
had(s), hold(s)
hae, have
haf, half
haffit, cheek

haflins, half
ha-house, farmhouse, "big house"
haik, hackney
hail the dools, go all out
hain'd, saved, stored
hair-mould, mouldy
hale, whole
halesome, wholesome
halland, inner wall or screen between door and fireplace
haly, holy
hame, home
hame-owr, at home
hameil, home-bred
hamely, homely
hamlock, hemlock
Handsel-Teysday, first Tuesday of the New Year
hap, happen
hap'd on, put clothes on
hap(pit), wrap(ped) (up)
hap-warms, wraps, thick garments
harl(in), drag(ging)
harpy, rapacious
har'st, harvest
hash, spoil, destroy
haugh, low ground beside a river
haveril, blethering
haw(s), hall(s)
hawkies, cows
hawses, throats
heart-scad, heartburn
hedge, protect
heeze, lift, raise
heid, head
herd, herdsman
herried, plundered
het, hot
hidling, hidden
hight, height, hill, raise
hinder, last
hiney, honey
hing, hang
hip, miss
hirpling, limping
hirsle, slip, slide
hive, haven
hobble, rock from side to side
hodin, homespun wool
hooly, cautiously
horse-cowper, horse-dealer
hotches, jolts
houff, haunt, shelter
houkit, dug
houp, hope
howder, swarm
howe, plain, flat land
howkit, dug
how-towdy, chicken for the pot
hummil, worn smooth
hund, hound
hunder, hundred
hungert, hungry
hurdies, buttocks
hurl, travel in a wheeled vehicle
hyn awa, away from here
idleseat, idleness
ilk, ilka, each, every
ill-hain'd, wrongly hoarded
ingan, onion
ingle, fireside, hearth
ingle cheek, fireside corner
ingyne, intellect
inlakes, lacks
inrow'd, enrolled
itlane (AG), itself

jaws, waves
jeels, jellies
jillet, flighty woman, flirt
jink, dodge, avoid
joe, sweetheart
jook, duck, avoid
joot, liquor
jow, toll
jumble, shake, disturb

kail, cabbage, vegetable broth
kail-worm, caterpillar
kail-yeard, kitchen garden
kaim, comb
kane, rent paid in kind
kebbuck, cheese
keek, look, peep, glance
keeking glass, mirror
ken, know
kendling, aflame
kent, shepherd's staff for leaping ditches
kep(pit), welcome(d)
kickshaws, delicacies
kill, kiln
kiltit, tucked up
kirn, churn
kirnstaff, the plunger of an upright churn
kist, chest
kist-nook, corner of chest reserved for valuables
kittle, tricky, difficult, cunning, uncertain
kniefly, with spirit
knowe, small hill
kye, cattle
kyte, belly
kyth, show, appear

labster, lobster

lade, load, fill
ladin(g), a load
laigh, low
laiglen, (milking) pail
lair, sink, lie
lair'd, buried
laith, loath
lake, lack
lammer-bead, amber bead
landlouper, vagabond
lanely, lonely
lang, long
lang syne, long ago
lanthron, lantern
lapper'd, curdled
lat, let
lathie, laddie
lave (the lave), the rest
laverock, lark
lawen, tavern bill, reckoning
leal, loyal, honest
leal, thoroughly
lear, learn
lee(s), lie(s), untruth(s)
lee-lang, livelong, entire
leem (Abdn), loom
lee-rigg, strip of grass
leesh, lash
leesins, lies
leet, list, register
leive (as leive), as well
lerroch, familiar place
ley-rig, see lee-rigg
lift, sky
lig, lie
lightlyin, despising, scornful
limmer, wench
lingans, threads
lintie, linnet
lippen, trust, expect

list, please
lith, joint
loo, love
loof, palm
loss, lose
Louden, Lothian
loun, lad, fellow
lounder, severe blow
loup, jump
lout, stoop, bend
lowe, blaze
lowse, loose
lug, ear, pectoral fin of a fish
luggie, small wooden vessel
lum, chimney
lure, rather
lyart, hoary, white-haired
lyther, more snug

macaroni, fop, dandy
mae, more
mailin, farm
mair, more
maist, most
maister-cann, vessel for holding urine
maister-laiglen, pail for urine
mament, moment
mane, moan, lament
'mang, among
maught, strength
maugre, in spite
maukin-mad, mad as a hare
maun(na), must (not)
maun (muckle maun), big (very big)
mavis, song-thrush
mead, meadow
meikle, much
meltith, meal

menzie, crowd, rabble
mergh, strength
mett, rhyme, match
mett, measured, paced
Mid-Louthian, Midlothian
mier (AG), moor
mirk, dark
mirlygoes, dizziness
misha(u)nter, misfortune, accident
mislear'd, ill-bred
mony, many
moose-wabs, cobwebs
motty, spotty, flecked
mou, mow, mouth
mou-bits, mouthfuls
mould, mouldy
muckle, great, large, much
multer, grain paid to miller for his services
musand, musing
mussel brose, mussels boiled in their own juices, mixed with oatmeal
mutch, a woman's cap

na, no, not
nae, no
naething, nothing
naig, horse
nakit, naked
nane, none
Nanesel (Her Nanesel), his own self (facetious name for a Highlander)
nappy, strong (of drink)
near-gawn, tight-fisted
neb, beak
neebor, neibour, neighbour
neist, next
newfangle, fond of novelty

nicker, neigh
nickstick, tally, reckoning-stick
nocht, nothing
noggan, noggin
nook, corner
Norland, northern
notar, notary, clerk
nouther, neither
nowt, cattle

obtemper'd, fulfilled
ohon (Gael), alas
ony, any
orra, odd, spare
ouk, week
owr, over, too
owrgang, outrun
owsen, oxen
oy, grandchild

pakes, strokes, blows
pandour, large oyster
pang'd, crammed
pap, pop
parritch, porridge
partan, crab
pat, pot
pat, put
paten, iron-mounted shoe
paughty, proud
pauky, **pawky**, cunning, lively
pease-clod, roll or loaf made from pease-meal
pech, gasp, pant
peel, call
peerify (AG), purify
perfite, perfect
phizz, face
pibrach, pibroch
pickle, little, small amount of

piddle, trifle
pig, chamber-pot, pitcher
pin, mood, humour
pingle, disagreement, difficulty
pirny, bobbin
pit, put
plack, small copper coin
plainstanes, pavement
plaisters, plasters
plash, splash
playfair, plaything
pleugh, plough, ploughman
pley, case
pley, dispute
plook, pimple, spot
plouky, pimply
pluck, feed, grazing
pock, purse
pomet, pomade, hair-oil
poortith, poverty, needs
pose, store of money
pow, head
powny, pony
prie(ve), taste, sample
prieven, tasting, sample
priggin, entreating
protty (Abdn), pretty
puddock, frog
purpie, purple
purpie-smiles, blushes

quat, quit
quean, lass
quegh, quaich
quo(d), quoth, said

raggit, rugged
raingit, lined up
rakin, rubbing
rangles, clusters

rantin blaze, roaring fire
ranting fu, roaring drunk
raw, row
rax, reach, stretch
ream, froth, foam
reath, period of three months
redd up, arranged
reek, reach
reesle, clatter
reid, red
reik, smoke, steam
remeid, remedy
respeckit, respected
riddle, sieve
rift, belch
rig(g), strip of ploughed land
riggin(g), back, roof
rigs, ridges between furrows
rin, run
ring, reign
ripe, search, rifle
rokelay, mantle, cloak
rook, the hindmost rook, the last farthing
rookit, rooked, robbed
roose, praise
roset, see **rozet**
roup, hoarseness
rout, rowt, roar, bellow
routh, plenty
rowe, roll
royit, wild
rozet, resin, or cobbler's wax
ruck, rick, stack
rug, pull, tear
rug (tak a rug), a good bargain
runcle, wrinkle
rung, staff

sae, so
saft, soft
sain, bless
sair, sore, sorely
sair'd, served
sall, shall
sang, song
sangster, songster
sappy, wet, slobbery
sark, shirt
sattlin, settling
saul, soul
saulie, professional mourner
saut, salt
sautit mart, salted bull or cow
sax, six
scad, scald
scald, scold
scancing, shining
scantlins, scarcely
scape, skep, hive
scar-craws, scarecrows
scart, scrape
scauld, scold
scaw'd, worthless
sclate, slate
scoug, see **scug**
scoup, scope
scour, cleanse, purge, run, rush about
scouth, room
scowder, scorch(ing)
scowry, blustery, showery
screech, shriek
screed, see **skreed**
scrimply, sparingly
scud, glide, flit, blow
scug, screen, hide
scunner, disgust, be disgusted
seed, seed-time
seenil, seldom

seeth(ing), boil(ing)
sel, self
sey, try, prove
sey-piece, show-piece
seything, see **seeth(ing)**
shake-winds, strong winds that shake the grain
shank, walk, leg, limb; **shank o' beer**, stem of beer, a long beer
shanna, shall not
sharger, runt of a litter
shaw, show
shaw, a small wood or thicket
she-doo, dove
shelly-coat, sheriff officer
shier (AG), sure
shoon, shoes
shour, shower
sib, closely related
sic, such
siccan, such
sicker, steady, secure
sien (AG), soon
siller, money, silver
simmer, summer
sin, since
skair, share, portion
skair, frighten off, take fright
skaith, harm, trouble
skaithless, unharmed
skate-rumple, back part of the skate
skelf, shelf
skelp, strike
skirl, cry out, shout
skreed, make a shrill sound, play loudly
slae-black, sloe-black
slaister'd, greased
slaisters, ointments
slavers, saliva, dribbles
slee(ly), skilful(ly), smooth(ly)
sleek, smooth
slocken, quench
sma, small, slender
smack, taste
smeek(it), smoke(d)
smore, smother
snaw(y), snow(y)
snell(y), keen(ly)
snodit, kept in order
sock, ploughshare
sock, sink
sonse, luck
sonsy, cheerful, fair
sough, hum, sigh
souk, suck
soum, float, swim
souple, pliant, supple, fluent
souter, cobbler
sowder, solder
sowf, whistle softly
sowl, soul
spae, foretell
spae-wives, fortune-tellers
spark, beau
spats, spots, markings
spatterdashes, gaiters
spaul, limb, bone
speal, time of relaxation
speel, climb
speen (AG), spoon
spelding, split smoked haddock
spence, inner apartment, retreat
spier, ask
spindle-shanks, thin limbs
spink, primrose, *or* pink
spraing, shade, colour
spraingit, variegated, brightly coloured

spreckled, speckled
springs, tunes
sprush, spruce
spulzie, spoil, plunder
spunk, spark
sta, stall
stamack, stomach, appetite
stane, stone
stang, sting
stap, stop, stuff
stappit, full, stuffed
stark, stout
starnie, star
staw, stow, stuff
steek, shut, close tight
steek, stitch
steeve, firm, steady
stegh, stuff, gorge
steid, stead, place
stent, lot, portion
stent, hurry
stey, steep
stirrah, fellow
stoiter, stagger
stoo, slice
stoup, flagon
stown, stolen
strae, straw
straik, stroke, blow
straught, straight
stravaig, roam, wander
streek, stretch, lay out
streen (the streen) (AG), see yestreen
sucker biskets, sugar biscuits
sud, should
suth'ron, southern
swack, supple, lithe
swaird, sward
swank, agile, active

sweel, swill
sweer, reluctant
swyth, quick, haste
syn', **synd**, wash, rinse, cleanse
syne, then, next, since

tack, lease
tack, fasten together
tae(s), toe(s)
taen, taken
tak, take
tane, (the) one
tap, top
targets, tatters
tassel'd, tattered
tassels, tussles
teats, small tufts
teem (Abdn), empty
teet-bo, peep-bo
tent, heed, tend
tenty, careful
thae, those
than, then
theekit, thatched
thegither, together
thereanent, concerning that
thereben, deep inside
thir, these
thof, though
thole, suffer, endure, tolerate
thornie-dike, hawthorn hedge
thoum, thumb
thraldom, bondage, care
thrang, throng, crowd(ed)
thrapple, windpipe, throat
thrave, thrived
thraw, twist
thrawart, bad-tempered, perverse
threap, **threep**, insist, boast

threave, a quantity of cut straw, usually two dozen sheaves
thristle, thistle
tift, (**in tift**), in good order, *also* windy
tig, whim, notion
til, to
tingle, ring, tinkle
tinkler, tinker
tint, lost
tirr, strip
tither, (the) other
todling, gliding, rippling
tongue-tackit, tongue-tied, silenced
toom, empty
toot, drink
toot aff the horn, drain the cup
tottl'd, boiled
touzle, tousle
towmonth, twelve-month, a year
treen, wooden
trig(ly), neat(ly), smart(ly)
trock, troke, do business, exchange, deal
troth, in truth
trou, trow, believe
truf(f), turf, grave
truncher, wooden platter
tulzie, trouble, tussle, fight
turner, copper coin worth twopence Scots
turnpike stair, spiral stair in a tenement
twa, two
twalt, twelfth
twin('d), deprive(d)
tyne, lose

ulie, ulzie, oil

uncanny, having supernatural powers
unco, uncommon, remarkable, very
unfleggit, unfazed, undismayed
unkend (to), unacquainted (with)

vacance, vacation
vaut, vault
viands, items of food
vockie, vogie, glad

wa, wall; **waas**, walls
wa'(s), way(s)
wad, wager
wad, would
wae, woe, sorry
waefu, woeful
waesuck, alas
wag, wave, nod
wale, the choice, best
wale their fitstaps, pick their steps
wallies, trinkets
walth, wealth
wamble, stir queasily
wame, belly
wanchancy, unlucky, dangerous
wanruly, unruly
wanwordy, worthless
wanworth, next to nothing
war, were
ware, spend
wark, work
warld, world
wat, wet
wat, know
wauken, waken
waukin, awake

waur, worse
weel, well, well-being
weelfardly, readily
ween, guess, imagine
weet, wet
weigh-bauk, balance
weir, war
weird, fate
weirlike, warlike
welkin, sky, region of clouds
well-a-day, lament
wether-gammond, leg of mutton
weym, see **wame**
weyr (Abdn), wire, i.e. knitting-needle
wha, who
whan, when
whang, cut, slice
whang, thong, strap
whar(e), where
wharewi, wherewith
whase, whose
whilk, which
whinge, whine
whisht, hush!
whitens, immature sea trout
whittle, blade, knife
whumble, turn upside down
whure, whore
wi, with
wie, a wee bit
wight, creature, person
wild-lorn, wild and waste

willawins, alas
win, dwell
windock, window
winna, will not
winnelstrae, withered stalk, straw
wirrikow, demon, bogle, the Devil
withouten, without
wizen, windpipe, throat
woo, wool
woodies, wooden poles
wook, week
wud, mad
wumill, wimble, gimlet
wun, win, gain
wyt (Abdn), know
wyte, blame

yae, one
yap, keen, hungry
yarkit, bruised
yeard, yard, earth
yelloch, yell, scream
yence, once
yestreen, last night
yill, ale
yird, see **yeard**
yole, small two-masted fishing-boat
yook, itch
youf, bark
younker, youngster
yowl, howl